HOW TO PLAY CHESS FOR KIDS

HOW TO PLAY
CHESS
FOR KIDS

SIMPLE STRATEGIES
TO WIN!

Jessica E. Martin

CALLISTO PUBLISHING

Cover Designer: Julie Schrader
Interior Designer: Antonio Valverde|
Art Producer: Janice Ackerman
Editor: Kristen Depken
Production Editor: Andrew Yackira
Production Manager: Giraud Lorber

Published by Callisto Publishing LLC C/O Sourcebooks LLC
P.O. Box 4410, Naperville, Illinois 60567-4410
(630) 961-3900
callistopublishing.com

This product conforms to all applicable CPSC and CPSIA standards.

Source of Production: Wing King Tong Paper Products Co.Ltd. Shenzhen, Guangdong Province, China
Date of Production: August 2023
Run Number: SBCAL112

Printed and bound in China.
WKT 14

This book is
dedicated to
my sweet son,
Albert, who is
my everything.

CONTENTS

NOTE FOR PARENTS

CHESS IS AN AMAZING GAME—some people even consider it a sport. It is both fun and competitive. As you probably know, there are incredible benefits for kids who play and study chess. Studies have shown that chess can improve test scores in school. Playing chess uses critical thinking skills such as higher-order thinking, memory, pattern recognition, math, and calculating abilities. It helps kids learn patience. It also teaches, through risk-benefit analysis, that there are consequences for each decision made. Children are exposed to social skills such as sportspersonship—learning to win with grace and lose with dignity. Every game begins and ends with a handshake (or a bow, if you're in my class). Kids may not even realize they are learning all these skills—they just have fun playing!

Chess should always be fun, and the goal of this book is to teach children how to play chess and have fun while doing so. Chess can be played by anyone, regardless of background or socioeconomic status, and at (almost) any age. Parents, you can learn along with your children or brush up on your skills! This book is designed to be accessible to elementary- and middle-school-aged children; however, you should spend some time going through part 1 (basics) and part 2 (tactics and strategy) with your younger children. If your children are ages 10 to 12, they may be more capable of working through the book independently. (Although I recommend you take a peek, regardless!) Kids love challenging their parents to a game. Read along to ensure you can still beat them! In my experience, parents who are involved in their children's learning of chess help their children learn more and retain more information. Remember to keep it fun!

WELCOME TO THE GAME OF KINGS AND QUEENS!

THIS BOOK IS YOUR KEY to learning to play chess. It will teach you the basics, explain some tricky rules, and show you some advanced strategies that will surprise your parents—and maybe even help you beat them!

My name is Jessica Era Martin. If you look me up, you'll find there is a scholarship named after me in Arizona, where I used to live and teach chess. I have also taught in New York City and North Carolina. I started teaching with my old coach many years ago and had so much fun! I love working with kids ages 4 through 14—from teaching how the pieces move to coaching them at National Championships. I used to be the number one–ranked woman chess player in North Carolina and have written another chess book, *My First Chess Book: 35 Easy and Fun Chess Activities for Children Aged 7 Years +* (under the name Jessica Prescott). So, I promise I know what I'm talking about. I love chess!

I first learned to play from my dad when I was five years old. I joined a chess club at my school and quickly learned how to beat my dad. This was a relief, because he used to sing a song when he checkmated me. It motivated me to compete and, when I was in second grade, I won the state championships for my grade.

All you're going to need is this book and a chess set (to practice), and you will learn to play and win! Did you know that chess makes you smarter? It does! You will get better at math and do better in school (even better than you already do! Is that possible?). With this book, you will learn how to play a legal, official game of chess—and you will even be ready for tournaments!

This book is split into two parts.

Part 1 is full of all the basics you need to start playing chess. It has some secret strategies, too—so even if you think you already know how to play, check it out!

Part 2 contains all the tactics and strategies that will help you win. (By the way, you don't win every time you play chess, but you do learn every time you play.) There are some secrets in here that I only teach my students!

Each section has step-by-step instructions and diagrams to help you follow along. I strongly suggest you get your chess set out to practice some of the tactics—especially when you get to the puzzles in the *Check it out!* sections in part 2. You may need to set up some of the positions to solve the quizzes. Take your time on these puzzles to make sure you really understand the answers! Read part 1 first, then, if you feel like it, you can skip around in part 2 to whichever tactic you feel like working on. Do each quiz immediately after you feel you understand the tactic. Of course, you could read everything in order, too. There is a glossary at the end of the book to review any new vocabulary (and there is a lot!).

Get ready to learn a fun game that will make you smarter and impress all the adults you meet.

PART ONE

How to Play Chess

In this section you will learn how the pieces move, the goal of the game, chess history, vocabulary (even in different languages!), and some basic chess strategies. Be sure to pay close attention to the diagrams. The section called *Checkmate!* is a summary of what you have learned in each chapter. You can always return to these sections if you need a reminder of something.

It is important to go through all of part 1—in order—to be prepared to understand part 2 completely. You will learn important rules like *castling*, *underpromotion*, and *en passant* (pronounced "on pah-sahnt"). Many people who say they play chess don't even know about these rules! Once you've got part 1 down, you'll be ready to take on the more challenging part 2.

1 LET'S START!

You need very little to play chess: just one person and a chess set! Actually, you could even go without the chess set if you have a great memory and want to play "blindfolded." Even though you win every time you play yourself, sometimes it's more fun to play against other people. So, let's say two people and a chess set are all you need. You could create your own chess set using toys or papier-mâché or any other objects—as long as you have enough different-looking and same-looking pieces. Be creative! Here's what you need to know about a chess set.

The Chess Set

I like using a professional set: a simple vinyl or silicone board and plastic or wooden pieces. But like I said, almost any set will do, as long as the board has 64 squares of alternating colors and the pieces are two different colors.

When you start a game, be sure the bottom row of the board has a *white square on the right-hand side.* It will be "white on the right" for both players. Otherwise your board is sideways! Your board may or may not have numbers and letters on it. These refer to the **files** (vertical rows) and **ranks** (horizontal columns). We say a, b, c, d, e, f, g, and h file when referring to the up-and-down columns. We say 1st, 2nd, 3rd, 4th, 5th, 6th, 7th, and 8th rank if we are talking about the rows going across the board. The letters and numbers are extremely useful when describing where a piece goes. This is the basis of a chess language, called **notation**, which we will get to later!

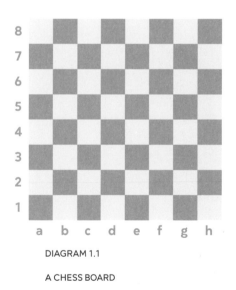

DIAGRAM 1.1

A CHESS BOARD

For now, you need to know that each square has a name: a first name and a last name. We call the first square in the left-hand corner of the player with white pieces a1. Its first name is "a" and its last name is "1." The square next to it is named b1. The square in the top right-hand corner of the board (again from the white side) is h8. White pieces always go on the 1st and 2nd ranks, and black pieces go on the 7th and 8th ranks. It's okay if you don't have letters and numbers on your board. In that case, all you have to do is be sure that the white square is on your right.

The pieces always start in the same spots. Each piece faces the **opponent's** piece. So, on the 2nd and 7th ranks, we place all eight white pawns and eight black pawns. The pawns are the little guys. They look like this:

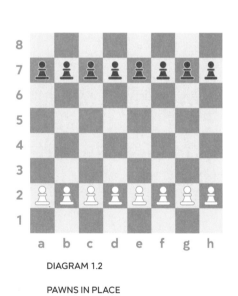

DIAGRAM 1.2

PAWNS IN PLACE

In each corner of the rank below the pawns, place a rook. They look like castles.

Next to the rooks, place the knights. They look like horses.

Next come the bishops on c1, f1, c8, and f8.

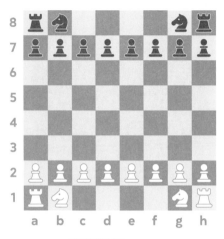

DIAGRAM 1.3

ADD THE ROOKS
AND KNIGHTS

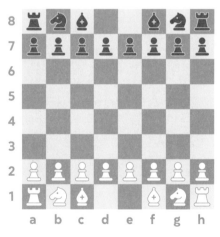

DIAGRAM 1.4

ADD THE BISHOPS

Notice that each player will have a bishop on a white square and a bishop on a black square. These are sometimes called "light-square bishop" or even "white bishop" (even if the piece color is black!).

Now for the super important stuff: the king and the queen! There are many people who confuse where these pieces are supposed to go. Here's how I always remember it: the queen goes on her own color. Light queen, light square; dark queen, dark square. You can think of the queen as wanting her shoes to match her dress.

The kings will face each other on the e file (see Diagram 1.5).

DIAGRAM 1.5

ADD THE KINGS AND QUEENS, AND YOU'RE READY TO PLAY!

Note: In professional sets, the king always has a cross on top, and the queen wears a crown. That's how they look in our diagrams, too. Note how you have eight pawns, two rooks, knights, and bishops, but only one king and one queen. Does your board look like the one in Diagram 1.5? Then you are ready to move on!

As in most games, you are supposed to take turns in chess. Black was traditionally considered the lucky color, so they let white go first. Make one move per turn. You keep taking turns until the game ends. (I'll tell you how the game ends in a minute.)

THE OLDEST GAME

Chess is one of the oldest games invented (or was it discovered?). Most people think it originated in India in the sixth century AD. So, it's older than baseball; it's older than Minecraft; it's older than the oldest game you can think of. Chess was called *Chaturanga* then, and some of the rules have changed since.

The Goal

The most important part of chess? How to win! Many people think you can capture the king in chess and that's how you win. Nope! You aren't allowed to capture kings in chess. *They never, ever, ever, ever, ever come off the board. They live there!* So, how do you win? **Checkmate!** Checkmate occurs when you have trapped the king and it cannot escape.

There are three possible results in a chess game: *win, lose,* or *draw*. If you checkmate your opponent, you win! Even if you have lost a lot of important pieces, **checkmate always wins**.

Along the way to checkmate, you're going to try to capture pieces and keep yours safe. If you can capture all of your opponent's pieces, you still haven't won, but it will be awfully hard for them to beat you. In fact, it will be impossible! You can't checkmate with only a king. That means, if there are only two kings left on the board, you've got yourself a **draw**! *A draw is a tied game*—no one wins; no one loses. There are lots of ways to make a draw. We will talk about some of them in more detail later.

Besides capturing pieces and keeping your pieces safe from capture, you'll need to keep your king safe from being attacked. There are strategies to do that. Pieces are important, but trapping the king (checkmate) wins the game. Sometimes you'll want to **trade** pieces (exchanging pieces of equal value) to help your **position**. Chess often comes down to position (where the pieces are—on particular squares—and the effect they are having on the other squares) and **material** (pieces). If you don't have a good position, your pieces can't help you at that moment. If you don't have any material, you can't create an attack.

You must try to get your pieces into better positions so you can create a checkmate. For this, you'll need a plan. We'll discuss methods of planning later.

ILLEGAL MOVES

In my classes, without fail, kids will tell me their family members are sure you can capture the king. It is a very common mistake! But trust me, it's against the rules. If someone tries to put their own king in danger, or forgets to get their king out of danger, this is called **illegal.** Yes, illegal! If someone says you can capture the king, tell them, "Checkmate wins!" It's the same if you try to make your pawn fly across the board and capture all the pieces, or try to use your king to make checkmate. These are all examples of illegal moves. You have to take the move back and try again.

CHECKMATE!

• •

Here is what you have learned in chapter 1:

☑ Set up your board with white on the right and each queen on her color.

☑ Use letters and numbers to describe where a piece should be placed.

☑ Take turns in chess.

☑ Checkmate wins—not capturing the king!

☑ Try to capture your opponent's pieces and keep yours safe.

☑ Attack your opponent's king and keep yours safe.

☑ Make a plan.

☑ Focus on position as well as material.

☑ You can win, lose, or draw in chess, but you should always have fun!

2 KINGS AND QUEENS AND MORE

Now it's time to learn how each piece moves. There are only six different pieces on the board, so this will be super easy for you! Each piece moves a certain way. You will discover what each piece is worth and learn some important strategies for playing with that piece. Each piece is special in some way! Piece values, or "points," help you figure out if and when you should make trades. I call points "cookies," because everyone (I think) loves cookies. You don't actually get any "points" (or cookies) from the pieces you've captured after the game is over. If you win, it's considered 1 point. A draw is considered ½ point, and a loss, well . . . 0 points.

The Pawn

Sometimes, when professionals talk about material, they do not consider pawns as pieces. But pawns are super important! Even though they are only worth 1 point, pawns can do something no other piece can do: *transform*!

MOVEMENT AND CAPTURES

Here are the four pawn rules you need to know:

1. Pawns always move forward.

2. Pawns only capture one square *diagonally* forward, which is different from how they move.

3. When a pawn is at its home base, where it starts the game, it may move one or two squares forward. After that, it may only move one square forward each turn.

4. When a pawn reaches the other side of the board, it may **promote** into any piece you want it to, except for a king. It cannot remain a pawn.

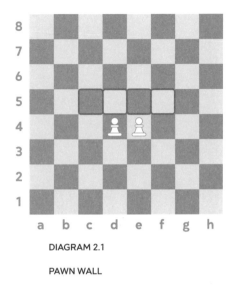

DIAGRAM 2.1

PAWN WALL

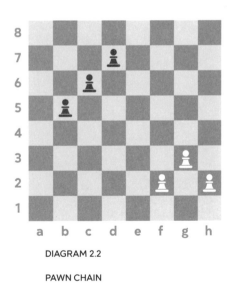

DIAGRAM 2.2

PAWN CHAIN

Therefore, when two pawns are head-to-head, they are frozen—and cannot move until another pawn or piece comes to a square diagonal from them so that they can capture it and "unfreeze!"

STRENGTHS AND STRATEGIES

Pawns have superpowers! Besides transforming, they can also capture pieces without touching them. What?! This is called **en passant.** (Skip to page 35 to see how pawns do this trick!)

Pawns like to stick together. When they are standing side by side, it's called a **wall.** See how the two pawns in Diagram 2.1 attack the four squares in front of them? Any piece that lands on one of those squares could be captured by one of the pawns.

Pawns also like to hold hands in a **chain.** When pawns are diagonal from each other, they protect each other! This is a very common pawn chain.

Look at Diagram 2.2. Black has a pawn chain where if someone captures the pawn on b5, the pawn on c6 could capture back. And if someone tries to capture c6, the pawn on d7 will be able to get it! Unfortunately, no one is guarding d7. He is called the **base of the pawn chain**, and, clearly, he is the weakest. (Even though he is doing important work!) White has two mini-chains: f2 is protecting g3, and so is h2. The pawn on g3 is probably feeling pretty confident right now.

What could white capture in Diagram 2.3? Do you remember the name of each piece? (Check back to pages 4–7 if you don't remember!) There are only two possible captures.

Did you remember that pawns capture one square diagonally away? And that pawns always go forward? Now look at Diagram 2.3 again. As white's pawns are moving up the board, only the pawn on c3 could take the queen on d4, and the pawn on h4 could capture the pawn on g5. Which one would you choose? Capturing the queen, of course! The pawn is only worth 1 point, but the queen is the most valuable piece on the board. Black's pawn on g5 could capture the pawn on h4 if it were black's turn.

DIAGRAM 2.3

THE PAWN ON c3 SHOULD
CAPTURE THE QUEEN
ON d4

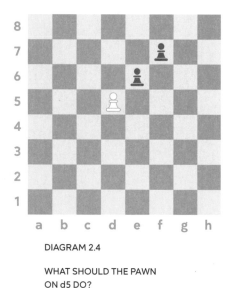

DIAGRAM 2.4

WHAT SHOULD THE PAWN
ON d5 DO?

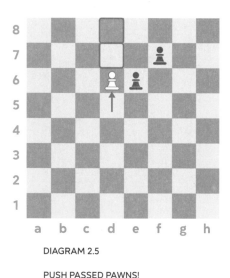

DIAGRAM 2.5

PUSH PASSED PAWNS!

Remember you can't capture backward and you can't capture two squares away. Pawns can move two squares from home, but they cannot capture two squares away ever.

Look at Diagram 2.4. What's the best move here?

Sure, you can capture the black pawn on e6. But you know what's better than capturing the pawn? Pushing forward! If you have a pawn with no opposing pawn in front of it, and no opposing pawn on either file next to it, that pawn is called a **passed pawn**. And you almost always *push passed pawns!* Don't forget, if your pawn reaches the other side, it can become a queen.

See Diagram 2.5. That pawn is a princess waiting to be crowned!

Try This Activity!

Set up only pawns. Now you can play a game of "pawn football." This is a race. Whoever can get a pawn to the other side first, wins!

The Rook

This is a strong piece. We call it a "heavy" piece. The rook is worth 5 points. It is the second most valuable piece next to only the queen.

MOVEMENT

It is super easy to learn how the rook moves. He can move forward, backward, and side to side as far as he wants! Make sure he goes in straight lines. And, although the rook can move in different directions, he can only move in one direction per turn.

STRENGTHS AND STRATEGIES

Rooks are like race cars that love to be on open freeways (files). When there are no pawns along a rook's path going forward, the rook controls the whole file!

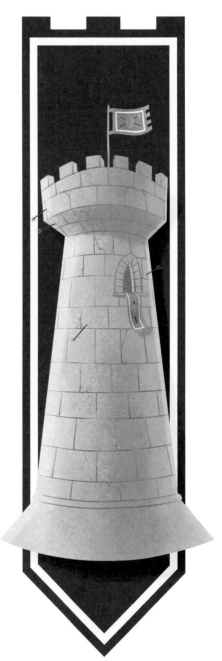

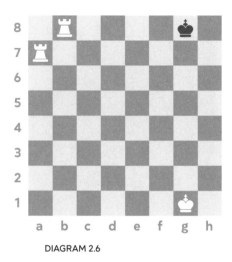

DIAGRAM 2.6

TWO ROOKS GUARD THE
7TH AND 8TH RANKS

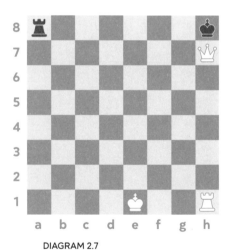

DIAGRAM 2.7

THE WHITE ROOK IS
BACKING UP THE QUEEN
IN A BATTERY

They are also powerful on ranks. In Diagram 2.6, look at the two rooks guarding the 7th and 8th ranks of the board. The king is trapped. Checkmate!

They also love to buddy up in a **battery** with another rook or a queen—this is when two pieces are lined up so they can work together. Batteries are superpowerful! In Diagram 2.7, the rook is backing up the queen—the black king cannot take the white queen, because the rook is in position to attack that **square**. This is one type of battery.

Each piece is special in some way. One of the unique things about the rook is that it can *castle* with the king. This is the only time the king can move two squares, and the only time the rook can jump! You will learn about castling in the next chapter.

The Bishop

Bishops are my second-favorite piece. They are worth 3 points—some people even consider a bishop worth a little bit more than 3. Bishops can create batteries with queens, too, but they are considered a "minor" piece (not a "major" or a "heavy" piece).

MOVEMENT AND CAPTURES

Bishops can move in diagonal lines as far as they want to. They can move one square, or as many as they want. Bishops capture the same way that they move.

Bishops cannot jump and they cannot change directions in one move.

STRENGTHS AND STRATEGIES

Bishops are especially good at attacking pieces in a row. Because bishops can go long distances, they are called **long-range pieces**. As long as there is

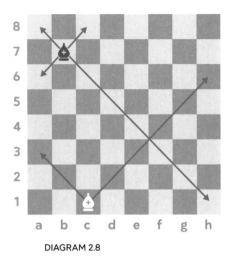

DIAGRAM 2.8

BISHOP MOVEMENT

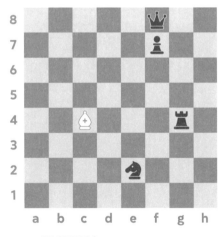

DIAGRAM 2.9

THE BISHOP SHOULD
CAPTURE THE KNIGHT
ON e2

a piece of the opposite color in their path, they can capture it. Bishops can't go through pieces on their own team, though. We're not playing ghost chess.

In Diagram 2.9, what should the bishop capture?

The bishop should capture the knight on e2! The knight is bigger than the pawn, so he is worth more. Plus, as you'll learn soon, the queen is actually guarding the pawn, so the bishop would get captured back. Notice that the rook is *not* guarding the knight, because rooks don't move diagonally. So, what would happen if the bishop stayed where it is? The rook would take it, of course!

Bishops are unique because they can create **pins** quickly and sneakily. They can also make **skewers**, batteries, and **discovered attacks** along with the other long-range pieces (the queen and the rook). You'll learn about these tactics and strategies in part 2.

In Diagram 2.10, the bishop is working with his friend, the queen.

This is checkmate! The queen is guarded by the bishop, and the queen cuts off all the king's escape squares. When the queen and bishop are lined up in the same rank, file, or diagonal together, that is a battery. This is also called a **helper mate**. Who's the helper? The bishop!

When two bishops are on adjacent diagonals, we call them **Horwitz bishops**. They can attack all the squares on the board because one attacks on white squares and the other attacks on black squares! Be careful when you trade bishops because they can be very useful. See Diagram 2.11.

This is checkmate, too! The black king in Diagram 2.11 is trapped because he can't put himself in danger by getting close to the other king. He can't stay where he is because of the bishop on b2. And he can't move over because of the bishop on c4. These bishops are not in a battery, but they are definitely working together!

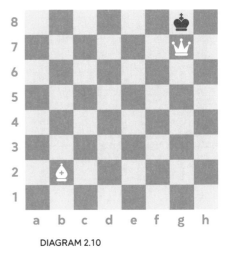

DIAGRAM 2.10

A HELPER MATE

DIAGRAM 2.11

HORWITZ BISHOPS

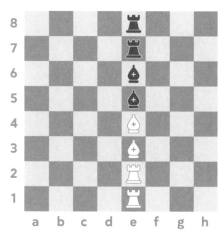

DIAGRAM 2.12

TRY THIS ACTIVITY!

Try This Activity!

Set up all the rooks and bishops on the e file as shown in Diagram 2.12. Whoever can capture their opponent's rooks and bishops first, wins!

DID YOU KNOW?

The bishop used to be called an elephant, and still is in many languages. It has a variety of names in different languages. For example, in French it is a jester, in Norwegian, a messenger, and in Mongolian, it's a camel!

The Queen

My favorite piece! The queen is the most powerful piece on the board. She is worth 9 points, and is also considered a "heavy" and a long-range piece.

MOVEMENT AND CAPTURES

The queen can move forward, backward, sideways, and diagonally! That means she moves like a rook and a bishop put together. She can capture any of the opposite-colored pieces in her way.

She still can't jump, though. And she doesn't move in circles around the board, so she can't exactly move in *any* direction.

STRENGTHS AND STRATEGIES

The queen is definitely the best piece for making checkmate! Because she can move in eight different directions, she can attack all the squares around the king when he is on the edge or the corner of the board.

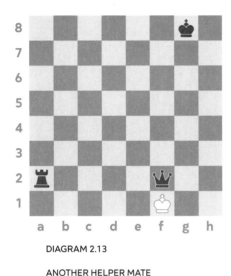

DIAGRAM 2.13

ANOTHER HELPER MATE

DIAGRAM 2.14

THIS QUEEN IS AIMING
AT FIVE PIECES

In Diagram 2.13, white is mated (mate is short for checkmate)! It's as if the black queen is giving the white king a big hug. She is looking right at him, and she guards all the squares around him, too. No escape! This is another helper mate. Who is helping this time? (The rook! The king may not capture the queen because he would be putting himself in check by the rook. You can never put your own king into danger.)

Queens are also good at **double attacks** because they can attack in so many directions!

Look at Diagram 2.14. The queen is aiming at five pieces! Do you know why I didn't add the black queen in her path?

(Because she'd be able to capture the white queen! See what would happen in Diagram 2.15.)

The queen is what most pawns promote to. Remember, you can promote a pawn to anything except the king (and it can't remain a pawn), but most people choose the queen. How many queens could there be on a chessboard for one side?

Well, if all your pawns promoted—and you still had your original queen—that would be nine! I've never seen that happen in a real game. Usually one or two queens will do the trick.

Queens are good at pins, skewers, and discovered attacks, all of which require a long-range piece. Some people like to bring their queen out early, in the **opening**. But she usually doesn't come out until the **middle game**, when you know on which side of the board you're going to focus your attack. The queen can be used for quick checkmates, but once your opponents learn your tricks, your queen will just get kicked around unless you use her carefully.

Look at Diagram 2.16. How can the queen make checkmate in this position? Give the king a big hug!

Either queen in Diagram 2.16 can go to c7, and the other will be protecting it to make a helper checkmate. The king won't be able to run or capture either queen, because the other queen will be

DIAGRAM 2.15

THE BLACK QUEEN WOULD
CAPTURE THE WHITE QUEEN

DIAGRAM 2.16

MAKE A HELPER CHECKMATE
IN ONE MOVE

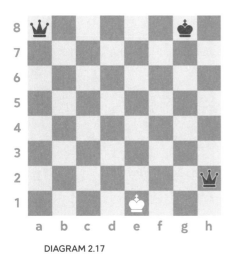

DIAGRAM 2.17

A CHECKMATE PUZZLE
WITH NO HELPER MATE

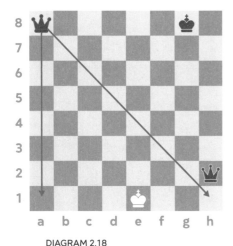

DIAGRAM 2.18

BACK RANK MATE

in place to attack it. We'll talk more about helper checkmates soon.

The queens could travel to black's back rank (the same rank its big pieces started on, the 8th rank) to attack the king, but he would still be able to run to d7 and/or b7, depending on which queen you chose. So, that wouldn't be checkmate, just **check**. Check is when the king is in danger, but he can escape.

In Diagrams 2.17 and 2.18, the queen on h2 is guarding the 2nd rank, so the king can't move forward. To trap him, you'll use the other queen to guard the 1st rank. The queen on a8 can go all the way down the board, either straight down or diagonally down. This is a **back rank mate!**

QUEENS RULE!

The queen wasn't always a queen. She used to be called the **vizier**, a male adviser to the king, and could only move one step diagonally. It wasn't until the fifteenth century when the Queen of Spain wondered, hey, where are all the ladies in this game? She decided the vizier should be a queen—and the most powerful piece on the board. This rule spread quickly and made the game a lot more exciting!

The Knight

Knights are unique pieces that work well with queens because they both have such distinct abilities. Knights are worth 3 points. That's the same as the bishop, remember, but knights are better at different things than the bishop.

MOVEMENT AND CAPTURES

This guy's tricky. You ready? The knight moves in an L shape. And the knight's special power is that it can jump! The way I think of the knight's move is to count out: zero, one, two, turn.

Look at Diagram 2.19. Do you see the capital L shape the knight makes? It would jump over red squares e4 and e3 and land on square f3. Even if there are pieces (white or black!) on red squares e4 and e3, it can jump over them. Because the knight can move in any direction, you can flip the L shape in any direction. That means the knight can actually move in eight different directions! He always

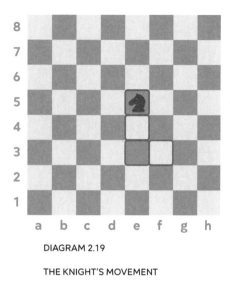

DIAGRAM 2.19

THE KNIGHT'S MOVEMENT

DIAGRAM 2.20

THIS KNIGHT CAN CAPTURE
ANY OF THE BLACK PAWNS

jumps: one, two, and turn. He cannot capture anyone he jumps over; he can only capture what he lands on at the end of his jump. If he isn't capturing anyone, he would land on an empty square.

Look at Diagram 2.20. The knight could capture any one of the black pawns! What shape do the pawns make? Isn't that a cool pattern? There are lots of patterns in chess. Knights are especially good at making interesting patterns.

STRENGTHS AND STRATEGIES

The knight is not a long-range piece. But it is fantastic at **double attacks** and **forks**. (You'll learn about those in part 2.) Because the knight can attack in such a sneaky way, people often won't realize that more than one piece is being targeted!

Knights are often better in **closed positions**. A closed position is one where lots of pawns are frozen (remember, that's when the pawns are head-to-head and can't move). That's because knights can hop around all the pawns. Bishops get stuck and have less freedom because the pawns are in their way.

The knight is also the only piece that can make a **smothered mate**. In a smothered mate, the king is trapped by his own pieces! Remember, sometimes position is better than material. In Diagram 2.21, the black knight could take the rook, which is more valuable in points, but what's better?

Checkmate, of course! It's kind of weird how the knight has to go away from its target sometimes. If the knight captured the rook, it would *not* be attacking the king. Knights *only* attack in an L shape, and they cannot attack their neighbors. But the knight is moving to a square that is an L shape away from the king, and the king is trapped by its own pieces (smothered). No one can capture the knight, and you can never block a knight check, so this is checkmate!

Why can't you block a knight's attack? You can't block a knight with another piece, because *the knight can jump right over it!*

DIAGRAM 2.21

A SMOTHERED MATE

The King

All right, I've saved the best and most important piece for last. You have already seen the king a lot in our examples. What keeps happening to him? Checkmate! That's how you win the game. You can't actually capture the king! Because of this, the king has no point value assigned to him. Some people say he is worth "infinity" or "the whole game" because when you checkmate the king, you win the whole game.

MOVEMENT AND CAPTURES

The king is a super-old man. Although he can move in any direction he wants to, he can only move one square at a time, and then he gets tired and has to stop.

He's so old and fragile, he doesn't want to head into battle with the rest of his pieces. So, in the beginning of the game, he hides in his castle and takes a nap. **Castling** is a special move the king can do with the rook. We'll get to the specifics of that soon.

The king can capture any piece that is one square away from him, *as long as he is safe there.*

STRENGTH AND STRATEGIES

At the end of the game, when most of the dangerous pieces are off the board, the king gets energized and becomes an attacking piece! He is especially useful at helping protect a pawn so it can promote safely.

In Diagram 2.23, the white pawn is about to promote on d8 and become a queen. Then it'll be lights-out for black! The black king cannot capture the pawn for a very important reason: *two kings never touch.*

If one king tried to get close to another king, we would call that illegal. It is illegal (against the rules) to put your *own* king into danger. Remember, he can't get captured. So, if you put your king in a position where he *could* be captured, **you have to take that move back**; it's simply not allowed. If your opponent makes an illegal move, tell them to take it back and try again.

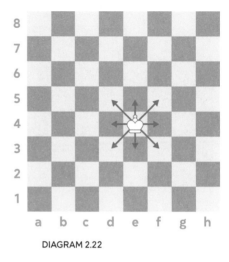

DIAGRAM 2.22

THE KING CAN MOVE IN ANY DIRECTION HE WANTS

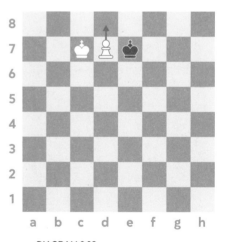

DIAGRAM 2.23

THE WHITE PAWN PROMOTES TO A QUEEN ON d8

DIAGRAM 2.24

THE BLACK KING IS IN
DANGER. WHAT CAN HE DO?

DIAGRAM 2.25

A QUEEN SANDWICH

Look at Diagram 2.24. The black king is in danger here. But he can't move to any of the empty squares around him because the queen would be aiming at him; she guards those squares. It would be illegal for the king to move there. What can he do?

He can capture the queen! No one is protecting her, so the king can easily take her off the board. Do you know what the result would be as soon as the black king captures the queen? A draw! Because two kings never touch, the game would end immediately as a tied game. The difference in the position in Diagram 2.25 is that the white king is protecting the queen, so the black king cannot capture her.

I call this a queen sandwich. It's checkmate! The white king is the bread, the queen is the cheese, and the black king is the bread . . . delicious! In checkmate, the king cannot move, no one can block, and no one can capture the piece that's attacking the king. He is trapped! We will practice more checkmates in chapter 3.

CHECKMATE!

Here is what you have learned in chapter 2:

☑ Pawns can move forward, capture diagonally, can move one or two squares from home (after which they can only move one), and can promote when they reach the other side of the board. When pawns are head-to-head, they are frozen.

☑ Rooks can move forward, backward, and side to side in a straight line.

☑ Bishops can move diagonally and always stay on the same color square they started on.

☑ Queens can move forward, backward, side to side, and diagonally.

☑ Knights move in an L shape and can jump.

☑ Kings move one square in any direction.

3 RULES TO REMEMBER

The following rules are very important! These rules will help you complete your basic chess knowledge so you can play a legal game. Now that you know how all the pieces move, you are ready to learn some critical chess ideas.

En Passant

En passant (pronounced "on pah-sahnt") is a way for pawns to capture *without even touching!* As you learned earlier, pawns always capture diagonally. That's still true, even when capturing en passant. If an opponent's pawn passes over your pawn's regular capture square, you can still capture it! Watch what happens in Diagrams 3.1–3.3.

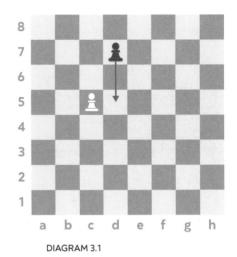

DIAGRAM 3.1

EN PASSANT: STEP 1

En passant is French for "in passing." Makes sense, right?

In Diagram 3.1, black's pawn is going to move two squares forward and land next to white's pawn, which you'll remember it can do (move two squares) from home. In doing so, it has just passed over white's regular capture square (see Diagram 3.2). Now white can take it!

DIAGRAM 3.2

EN PASSANT: STEP 2

DIAGRAM 3.3

EN PASSANT:
FINAL POSITION

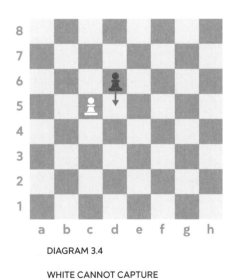

DIAGRAM 3.4

WHITE CANNOT CAPTURE
EN PASSANT

Look at Diagram 3.3 to see your final position. White has captured the black pawn using en passant! It's as though the black pawn had only moved one square forward. If it had gone only one square, it could have been captured. If it goes two squares it can *still* be captured. (If white wants to—you don't always have to capture things, but it looks like a pretty good move in this example.)

There are two questions to ask when capturing en passant:

1. Are our pawns side by side?

2. Did my opponent's pawn *just* move two squares?

If the answer to both of these is yes, your pawn can capture the other pawn! Only pawns can use this rule. This is tricky! You absolutely have to say yes to those two preceding questions in order to do it. If the pawn only moves one square, and you're side by side at that point, you *may not* use en passant.

Look at Diagram 3.4. Black just moved from d6 to d5, one square. (It probably should have captured the white pawn, but it didn't.) White cannot capture en passant.

In Diagram 3.5, these two pawns are frozen. They cannot capture each other.

If your opponent moves their pawn two squares forward and lands next to yours, and you decide *not* to capture en passant, then you lose your opportunity to capture it next turn, even if they're still in the same position. *You have to do en passant immediately*—as soon as your opponent moves two squares—if you want to use it.

In Diagram 3.6, the pawns are side by side, but black has just moved the knight. No en passant!

DIAGRAM 3.5

THESE PAWNS ARE FROZEN

DIAGRAM 3.6

NO EN PASSANT BECAUSE BLACK HAS JUST MOVED THE KNIGHT

Try This Activity

Play a game with only pawns, like the pawn football game (see page 16), but include the possibility of en passant!

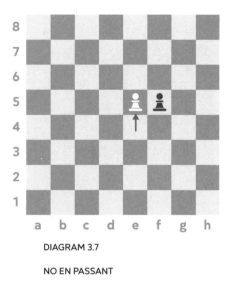

DIAGRAM 3.7

NO EN PASSANT

DIAGRAM 3.8

EN PASSANT IS OKAY!

You try one. Look at Diagram 3.7. Can black capture the white pawn using en passant?

White just moved to e5. No en passant! White only moved one square forward, not two. Next, look at Diagram 3.8. How about now?

White just moved to e4. Yes! Black can capture en passant. It doesn't matter that there is a knight on f3. The black pawn would land on e3 and the white pawn would disappear!

As long as the opposing pawn has just moved forward two squares and landed next to your pawn, any of your pawns can use this rule.

Check

Check: If your king is in check, he is in danger! You *must* save your king, if possible. There are three ways to try to get out of check—you can *move, block, or capture*. That's it! I remember it as MBC. Some people think of it as CPR: capture, protect, run. Think of it however you want. Remember that kings never come off the board, so if your king is in danger, save him!

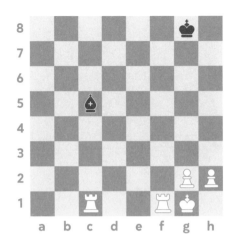

8 | | | | | | | ♚ |
7 | | | | | | | |
6 | | | | | | | |
5 | ♝ | | | | | |
4 | | | | | | | |
3 | | | | | | | |
2 | | | | | ♙ | ♙ |
1 | ♖ | | | ♖ | ♔ | |

a b c d e f g h

DIAGRAM 3.9

GET OUT OF CHECK BY
USING YOUR ROOK ON c1
TO CAPTURE THE BISHOP
ON c5

Any piece can put a king in check except the other king!

Check is not checkmate. But what if there is no legal move? No way to get out of check safely? That *is* checkmate. We'll get into this more in a moment.

Look at Diagram 3.9. You can choose how to get out of check. Do you see the black bishop aiming at the white king? You can move your king to h1, out of the bishop's reach; you can block by putting your rook on f2, getting in the bishop's way; or, you can capture the bishop using your rook on c1. Which is best? Capturing, of course! Always look for ways to capture to get out of check. Even the king can capture if a piece is too close and unguarded.

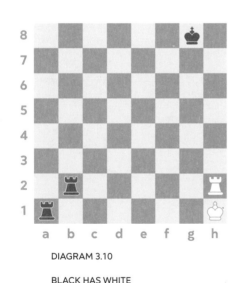

DIAGRAM 3.10

BLACK HAS WHITE
IN CHECKMATE

Checkmate

Checkmate: Game over! You can see the word "check" inside "checkmate"—that means the king must be in danger of checkmate. The "mate" part means the king *cannot* move, block, or capture to escape! Let's look at the example in Diagram 3.10.

The black rook on a1 is checking the white king. The white rook can't help out at all. The king can't move out of the rooks' paths, no one can block, and nothing can capture the rook on a1. Checkmate! This is a **ladder mate** (also a **back rank mate**). You'll learn how to make a ladder checkmate in chapter 4!

There are lots of different checkmating patterns. My favorite one is called a *swallow's tail*. Think of a swallowtail bird, or a butterfly, and the way its tail splits into two parts. Now look at Diagram 3.11.

The queen is the head and the pawns are the tail! The white king cannot escape to any safe square.

You've seen the helper mate and the queen sandwich and the ladder mate. Those are the most common checkmates; there are many more. See if you can solve these next few checkmate-in-one puzzles. (Turn to the Quiz Answers section, page 121, to check your answers.)

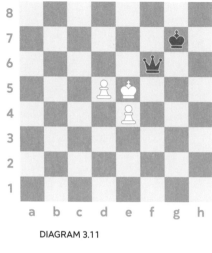

DIAGRAM 3.11

THE SWALLOW'S TAIL
CHECKMATE PATTERN

Quiz 1. White to move and checkmate in one move.

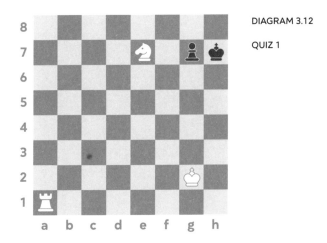

DIAGRAM 3.12

QUIZ 1

Quiz 2. Black to move and checkmate in one move.

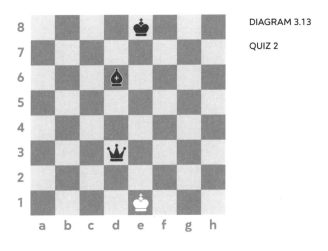

DIAGRAM 3.13

QUIZ 2

HOW TO PLAY CHESS FOR KIDS

Quiz 3. White to move and checkmate in one move.

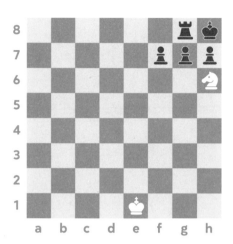

DIAGRAM 3.14

QUIZ 3

Quiz 4. White to move and checkmate in one move.

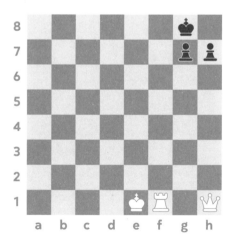

DIAGRAM 3.15

QUIZ 4

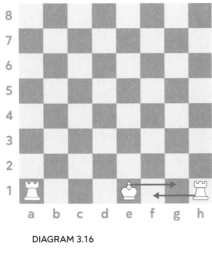

DIAGRAM 3.16

CASTLING KINGSIDE

DIAGRAM 3.17

FINAL CASTLED POSITION

Castling

Castling: This is a great strategy that only the king and rooks can do. The king will move two squares toward either rook, and that rook will jump over the king! This is an important way to protect your king. The king is sort of lazy at the beginning of the game. And most of the time he should hide in his castle. There he takes a nap until it's time to wake up!

Let's look at Diagram 3.16. The king gets to move two squares toward the rook (here he has chosen to castle **kingside** or "short"). That means he has moved on the king's side of the board. The rook JUMPS over the king and lands right next door! This is the *only* time in chess when your king can move two squares and your rook can jump. Look at Diagram 3.17 for the final castled position.

Now look at Diagram 3.18. Here, the king castles on the **queenside** or "long." He moves toward the queen's side of the board. Even though she isn't there now, the queen started on d1, so that is her half of the board.

The king still moves two squares toward the rook, and the rook still jumps over the king and lands right next to it. Black can castle, too, of course.

There are five times you **cannot** castle. You cannot castle if:

1. You are in check.
2. You would have to go through check to castle.
3. You would land in check.
4. Your king or castling rook has already moved.
5. There are pieces in your way.

Look at Diagram 3.19. Black is in check and, therefore, can't castle at all. White can't castle queenside because the bishop on g4 is attacking d1, so the king would be going through danger. White can castle kingside safely. And for black to get out of check, his pawn should take the knight.

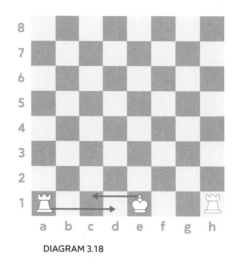

DIAGRAM 3.18

CASTLING QUEENSIDE

DIAGRAM 3.19

BLACK IS IN CHECK

You should castle within the first 10 moves, usually.

DIAGRAM 3.20

UNDERPROMOTION

Promotion

Promotion: When a pawn reaches the other side of the board, it can be promoted to any other piece—it just can't become a king or remain a pawn. We looked at this in chapter 2. But here is something special we haven't talked about yet. Usually it's best to promote the pawn to a queen, because the queen is the most powerful piece. But sometimes a smaller piece is better for the position.

This is called **underpromotion**. Look at Diagram 3.20 for an example.

Those are powerful pawns! You should promote to a knight here to make an immediate check-mate—the knight would be in the perfect position to attack the king. If you were to promote to a queen, you'd actually get a **stalemate**, which is a type of draw!

CHECKMATE!

. . . .

Here is what you have learned in chapter 3:

☑ En passant is a way for pawns to capture other pawns that have passed over their regular capture square.

☑ "Check" means the king is in danger. You must move, block, or capture (MBC) to get the king safe.

☑ "Checkmate" means the game is over, and you win! Your opponent cannot move, block, or capture to escape from check.

☑ Castling is a way to try to protect the king. The king moves two squares, and the rook jumps over and lands right next to the king. You should try to castle early in the game.

☑ Promotion happens when a pawn reaches the other side. It can become any piece it wants, even if that piece hasn't been captured yet, except for a king or a pawn.

4 STAGES OF THE GAME

There are three parts of a chess game: the **opening**, the **middle game**, and the **endgame**. In this chapter we will learn basic strategies for each stage.

Opening

There is no specific number of moves that makes something an opening. It can be the first move, or the first 21 moves! It means *how* you start your game—which pawns or pieces you move first. That will indicate what opening you have chosen. Each opening has a name (unless you've made something up, which is perfectly fine when you start out as a chess player). And there are loads of different openings, all with different names and variations. The names are either countries or last names of the people who perfected the opening. For example, the English is my favorite opening for white. But some people start out with the Réti (named after Richard Réti—you'll be ready for anything!). You could read a thousand books just on openings and opening theory! We will focus on the goal, which is to get your pieces out to good squares and get ready to castle.

The theory is that there are three things you should *always* (okay, *almost always*) do in the opening: CDC!

1. Center

2. Develop

3. Castle

Center means to aim your pawns and pieces at the center of the chessboard. The four center squares are d4, d5, e4, and e5.

Develop means to bring your pieces out from the back rank. (Not the king, though.)

Once you're mostly developed, you can castle! Diagram 4.1 shows a good example of pieces being developed toward the center.

I call this the **rainbow opening**. Do you see the rainbow?

You should develop your pawns, knights, and bishops first. That gives you a chance to castle quickly on the kingside. If you want to castle queenside, all you have to do is move the queen as well and there you go! I didn't give black any moves in Diagram 4.1, but if I had, and black were moving

DIAGRAM 4.1

THE RAINBOW OPENING

toward the center, you probably wouldn't be able to get all your pieces into the rainbow position safely.

The Italian opening (an opening for white) is what I teach my students when they are ready for it. Are you ready? Look at Diagram 4.2 and try these three moves:

First, move the pawn toward the center, then the knight on his happy square (that means toward the center, not the side). Then the bishop comes out to c4 so that it can aim at f7, the weakest square on the board. Now you are ready to castle and attack! I did not give black any moves here as we are just looking at ideas for white.

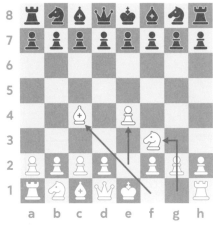

DIAGRAM 4.2

THE ITALIAN OPENING

THE WEAKEST SQUARES

F7 is the weakest square for black, and f2 is the weakest square for white, before castling. Only the king is guarding that square. It is very dangerous for him. Never move your f-pawn unless I have given you written permission!

Middle Game

This is the stage of the game where both sides have developed most of their pieces and have castled. Now you get to attack! You'll use the tactics in chapter 6 and the strategies in chapter 7 to do this.

The most important thing at this point in your chess career is to make sure you use all your pieces, not lose all your pieces. This is going to require that you look ahead and ask yourself, "If I place my piece there, will it be **hanging** or **protected**?" If a piece is hanging, no one is guarding it, and it can be captured for free, without being captured back. Protected is the opposite of hanging. If you capture it, you will get captured back. When your opponent places a piece down, ask yourself, "Is it hanging or protected?"

In order to use all your pieces, they will need freedom! Instead of cramping up your pieces, which is more defensive, try to bring them out toward the middle.

Now you need to make a plan. That means, go for an attack somewhere on the board! I suggest going for the king, but sometimes the position requires a different plan. Whenever I'm not sure what to do, I ask myself which piece is not **active**—or participating in the game and doing a job—and I try to get it to a better square. You want your pieces to work together harmoniously! You'll see a good example of this in chapter 7.

Look at Diagram 4.3. Which of white's pieces hasn't moved yet? The rook on h1! Do you see a nice open file for it? That's right: move to d1! This is from a famous game played by Paul Morphy, the first unofficial World Chess Champion. He had white and he won very quickly.

DIAGRAM 4.3

MOVE THE ROOK ON h1 TO d1 TO MAKE IT ACTIVE

GUESS WHAT?

Paul Morphy was playing the just-mentioned game against two players! The Duke of Brunswick and Count Isouard played Morphy at an opera house in Paris in 1858. It's one of my favorite games to teach. Check out where you can find it in the Resources section on page 128.

Endgame

You are in the endgame when the queens come off the board. Sometimes, if the queens are still there but most of the other pieces have been traded off, it's still an endgame. The key element of the endgame is that most of the pieces are gone. You'll need to know how to win at this point.

If the queens have been traded off the board, your goal is to promote!

If you don't have pawns to promote, but you do have two rooks against a lone king, you can use the ladder mate to win, which I'll show you shortly. If you have a queen against a lone king, you can use the queen dance to win—super fun stuff!

Next are two techniques you can use to force a checkmate in the endgame.

THE LADDER MATE

In the ladder mate (also called a back rank mate), you'll use two rooks (or a rook and a queen, or two

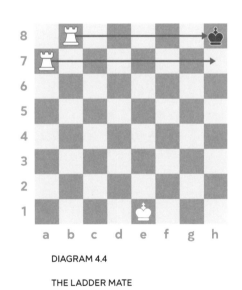

DIAGRAM 4.4

THE LADDER MATE

queens) to force the king to the back rank. Look at Diagram 4.4 to see what your final position could look like.

The rook on b8 gives check and cuts off the entire back rank; the rook on a7 cuts off all the escape squares on the 7th rank. This is a **pattern**. That means your board could look slightly different—the mate could be on the side files or the first rank, and your rooks could be in different spots. As long as one guards the back rank and the other guards the escape squares, you're golden.

How do you do it? I like to think of the king as a bug, and the rooks as feet. You need to sweep the bug down the stairs to the front door. You don't want the bug to bite you, and you don't want to step on it! So, you'll just push him farther and farther away, until he can fly out the front door, or the window, or whatever.

All you do is walk! Look at Diagram 4.5. The rook on a1 is your back foot; the rook on b2 is your front foot. Start walking toward the king.

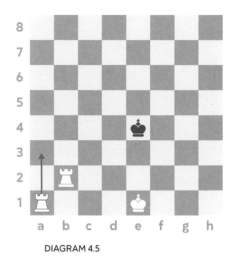

DIAGRAM 4.5

START WALKING YOUR ROOKS TOWARD THE KING

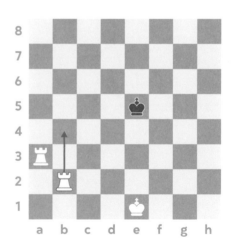

DIAGRAM 4.6

MOVE YOUR BACK FOOT FORWARD TWO SQUARES

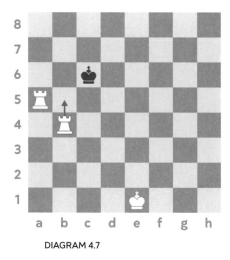

DIAGRAM 4.7

MOVE YOUR ROOK UP
ONLY ONE STEP

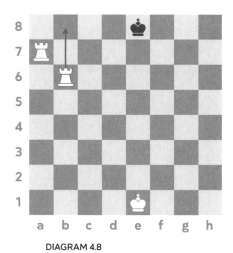

DIAGRAM 4.8

WHITE CAN MOVE AND
MAKE CHECKMATE IN
ONE MOVE

The king won't be able to come down, so he can go sideways or up. Let's keep pushing him back toward the door!

Just move your back foot two steps forward!

Look at Diagram 4.6. Do you see a pattern? Your back foot will go two squares forward each time! There is only one thing the bug can do to try to be tricky. It can come straight for your toes!

If that happens, you buddy up. Bring your back foot up one step instead of two. The rooks are in a battery and guard each other. No toe biting today!

Now look at Diagram 4.7. Do you see how, if you follow the previous pattern (of moving two squares with your back foot), the king will simply capture your rook? There would be nothing guarding it. Instead, move your rook up only one step, as shown. Buddies!

Then you can continue guarding one rank at a time. If one of your rooks is guarding the 5th rank, move the other to guard the 6th rank. When the king moves away you can follow the pattern again.

Back foot forward two steps. Now white can make checkmate in one move! See Diagram 4.8.

Bye-bye, buggie! If the bug is being super annoying and staying at your toes, and buddying up doesn't seem to work, you can also do the splits! Watch what happens in Diagram 4.9.

You're already buddied up. You can't move either rook forward without the b-rook getting captured. Do the splits! If the bug stays near your other foot, get back into walking position on the far side of the board. See Diagram 4.10. Now the bug can't reach you, and you can walk forward on your next turn.

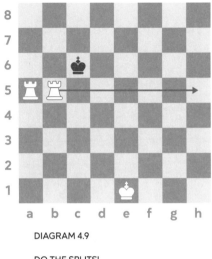

DIAGRAM 4.9

DO THE SPLITS!

Try This Activity!

Practice this by yourself or with a friend. Start with both rooks in any of the two corners of the board. Place the king of the opposite color anywhere on the board. Get your feet into walking position and go from there! Be sure to watch for illegal moves.

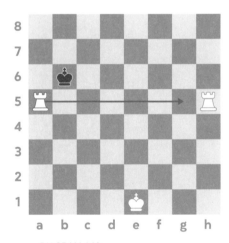

DIAGRAM 4.10

GET BACK INTO WALKING POSITION ON THE FAR SIDE OF THE BOARD

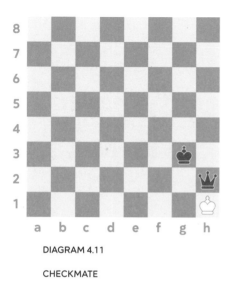

DIAGRAM 4.11

CHECKMATE

THE QUEEN DANCE

To learn the queen dance, you'll need a brief overview of what **stalemate** is. A stalemate is a type of draw where the king is *not* in check, but there are no legal moves on the board. The king is trapped and can't move, and neither can his other pieces, if there are any.

CHECK	MATE	STALE	MATE
The king is in danger. You can move, block, or capture.	You cannot move, block, or capture to escape—a win/loss.	The king is NOT in danger.	You cannot move, block, or capture to escape—a draw.

Diagram 4.11 shows an example of a *checkmate*. It's white's turn, they're in check, but can't move anywhere safely!

Diagram 4.12 shows an example of a *stalemate*. It is white's turn, they're *not* in check, but can't move anywhere safely!

Note that if there were another white piece on the board that could move, it would *not* be

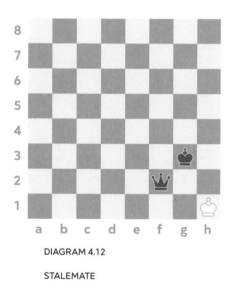

DIAGRAM 4.12

STALEMATE

stalemate. It would just be a regular position and white would move that piece.

Time to dance!

1. Get your queen a knight's distance away from your opponent's king. (No, she doesn't move like a knight. She's just an L shape away from the king.) See Diagram 4.13.

DIAGRAM 4.13

THE QUEEN DANCE: STEP 1

2. Now you get to follow the king wherever he goes! He will never be able to escape the box you've created around him. If the king goes one square diagonally down and to the right, the queen goes one square diagonally down and to the right. See Diagram 4.14.

The box around the king will keep getting smaller until he reaches the corner. Then you stop: red flashing lights! Don't follow the king into the corner or you'll make a stalemate.

Look at Diagram 4.15. The king is trapped in a small box. The red squares show all the places the queen guards around the king.

DIAGRAM 4.14

THE QUEEN FOLLOWS
THE KING

DIAGRAM 4.15

THE KING IS TRAPPED BUT STILL
HAS ONE SQUARE TO MOVE TO

DIAGRAM 4.16

CHECKMATE IN ONE MOVE!

3. Now you bring in your king! All white can do is sadly pace back and forth until the black king is close enough to make a helper mate, or a queen sandwich! Look at Diagram 4.16. I've skipped a few more moves and now the king has come close enough for checkmate! Where is it? There are five different checkmating moves. Can you find all of them? (Turn to the Quiz Answers section to see what they are.)

Note that if you have only a knight, or a bishop, or even two knights, you can't *force* checkmate. And in those situations, if the pawns have all been captured, you will get an automatic draw due to **insufficient mating material.** You can win with a queen, two rooks, one rook, two bishops, sometimes a knight and bishop (although it's ridiculously hard, so it's totally acceptable to call it a draw), and sometimes with a pawn if the position is good. (Because the pawn will promote to a queen and you'll do the queen dance!)

CHECKMATE!

· ·

Here is what we have learned in chapter 4:

☑ CDC in the opening—that is, develop your pieces toward the center so that you can castle.

☑ After your pieces are developed and you are castled, you are ready to attack using tactics and strategies.

☑ Try to promote a pawn in the endgame. If you have rooks and/or a queen, you can force a checkmate using these techniques: ladder mate or the queen dance.

☑ Be careful about stalemate. This type of draw occurs when the king is not in check but there are no legal moves on the board for the person whose turn it is.

5 CHESS NOTATION

Notation is really cool! It's like learning a new language—a chess language! You'll need to know it to follow the tactics and strategies coming up in part 2. But it's also super important for a few other reasons.

Why Notate?

We'll discuss the reasons notation is important in this chapter, and then show you how to notate. First, if you notate, you can review the entire game afterward! That means you'll be able to show off your amazing tactics, learn from your mistakes, and learn things from your opponent as well.

Second, you may need notation in a tournament to prove things like whose turn it is, or if a position has repeated itself three times (**threefold repetition of position** is another type of draw), or if 50 moves have passed without a capture or a pawn move (the **50-move rule** is another type of draw).

Third, it will help you analyze Grandmaster (or GM) games that have been notated. "Grandmaster" is the highest level of chess player you can become. (Well, there are Super Grandmasters, but that's an unofficial term to describe the best of the best.) Imagine how much you can learn from these GMs!

How It Works

You already know the names of the squares. Remember, they have a first and a last name (a letter, then a number). All you need to know now is how to identify the pieces and a few other symbols. It's super easy! The king, queen, rook, and bishop are identified by the first letter of their names. The knight and pawn are different. We don't want to confuse the knight with the king, so even though knight starts with a silent k, we use the first letter we hear, the N, to describe it. Pawns, poor little guys, don't get a letter at all. When you see notation that only shows the name of the square, with no piece specified, that means a pawn is on that square.

King	K
Queen	Q
Rook	R
Bishop	B

Knight	N
Pawn	(no letter, just the square name)

The table that follows is an example of how to write down the first three moves of the Italian opening we looked at earlier. You would write down both white's and black's moves. Diagram 5.1 shows the Italian opening.

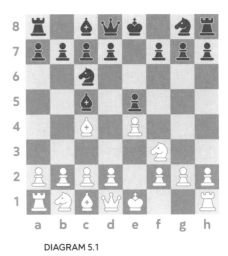

DIAGRAM 5.1

THE ITALIAN OPENING

White	Black
1. e4 (pawn to e4)	e5 (pawn to e5)
2. Nf3 (knight to f3)	Nc6 (knight to c6)
3. Bc4 (bishop to c4)	Bc5 (bishop to c5)

When two pieces can go to the same square, we need to identify where the piece started, so we know which piece to move. Look at Diagram 5.2.

It's black's move in this **Queen's Gambit Declined, Semi-Slav opening**. Black would like to put the knight on d7. But both knights can go to d7, so how should we indicate which one? We use the letter

DIAGRAM 5.2

QUEEN'S GAMBIT DECLINED, SEMI-SLAV OPENING

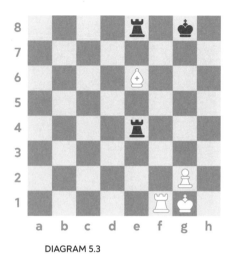

DIAGRAM 5.3

BOTH ROOKS CAN
CAPTURE THE BISHOP

where the knight started, so Nbd7. That means the knight that was on b8 goes to d7. (Not the knight on f6.) If two pieces of the same type are on the same file and can go to the same square, we would use the number to identify which piece moves there.

Look at Diagram 5.3. Both rooks can capture the bishop. If you wanted to use the rook from the back rank, you would notate it like this: R8xe6 ("x" in this notation indicates a capture). If you were to use the rook on e4, you would say: R4xe6. Make sense?

Here are the other symbols you'll need to know:

Castling kingside	0-0 (glasses!)
Castling queenside	0-0-0 (an alien with glasses!)
Piece capturing anything	x in between piece and square it landed on (example: Nxe5)
Pawn capturing a piece	x in between letter of file where pawn started and square it landed on (dxe5)
Pawn capturing a pawn	letter of file where pawn started then letter of file where pawn landed (de)
Check	+ at the end of the notation (Bxf7+ means the bishop captures on f7 and makes check)

Double check (when two pieces give check at the same time)	++ at the end of the notation (Nh6++)
Checkmate	# at the end of the notation (Qxf7#)
Promotion	square where pawn landed, equal sign, first letter of piece you promoted to (c8=Q)
Black's move	ellipses are used to indicate it's black's move, if white's move is not mentioned first. (1 ... e5)

Some chess books do notation differently, but this style is called *algebraic notation*. It is the most current and professional notation used. All professionals write their moves down. You should try it, too!

Try This Activity!

Play a game! Write down at least the first five moves. After you feel comfortable, try to write down 10 moves then, next time, the whole game!

Get out your chess set and play through the moves from this awesome game played in the year 1620. How do we know what moves they made? They notated! (Except for the name of the person playing as black . . .)

White	Black
Gioachino Greco	No name recorded
1. e4	e5
2. Nf3	Qf6
3. Bc4	Qg6
4. 0-0	Qxe4
5. Bxf7+	Ke7
6. Re1	Qf4
7. Rxe5+	Kd8
8. Re8#	

There is a lot we could discuss about this game, but you'll notice that white played the Italian opening. And black used his queen way too much, and too early in the opening.

CHECKMATE!

· ·

Here is what you learned in chapter 5:

☑ Notation is important because you can prove what happened in your game, and you can review it afterward.

☑ Each piece's name starts with a capital letter, except for pawns.

☑ Captures, checks, castling, and pawn promotion have special ways of being notated.

☑ You can read a fully notated game. Now you know a new language!

PART TWO

Ways to Win

Now that you know how to play a legal game of chess, you are ready to learn **tactics** and **strategies** to win the game! *Tactics* are ways to forcibly win material or get a quick checkmate. Sometimes they are used in a **combination** (two or more tactics put together). *Strategies* are methods of putting your pieces on certain squares to improve your position. Remember: Chess is a mixture of material and position.

Because you don't want to just make **hoping moves**, crossing your fingers that your opponent will make a terrible mistake and help you win, you'll need to make **forcing moves** to make sure you win. These are the supersecret tricks I teach my students, so don't tell your opponents your plans!

6 TERRIFIC TACTICS

Here you will learn about tactics. Tactics are tricks to win! You will learn about forks, pins, skewers, discovered attacks, double checks, remove-the-guard, sacrifices, decoys, and deflections. If you would like to skip around, that's fine, but be sure to cover all the different tactics. Note that there will be a quiz at the end of each tactic so you can start to recognize the patterns.

To find any tactic, you first have to identify where the **hanging pieces** are. A hanging piece is completely unprotected—no one is guarding it, so it could be captured for free, without getting captured back. Follow these tactics to see how you'll be able to capture it on your next move.

Fork

A fork is a funny way of saying you are attacking two or more pieces at the same time. Think of a fork in the road or a snake's tongue!

Some people call forks "double attacks." A double attack can include attacking a piece and an empty square. Why on earth would you attack an empty square? Because maybe on your next move you would go there to make checkmate! When you attack two pieces, you'll (usually) be able to capture one. That's because no one can save two pieces by moving both away at the same time. Look at Diagram 6.1 to see what I mean by a fork.

The black knight attacks both the king and the queen! You are attacking the most important pieces and white can't save both. White absolutely needs to save the king because he is in check. Remember you escape from check by using MBC (move, block, or capture), so white will be forced to move the king. (There is no way to capture the knight or block

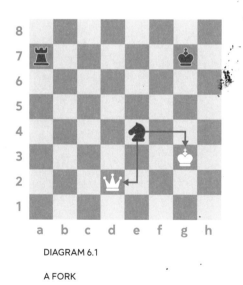

DIAGRAM 6.1

A FORK

the check.) Once white moves the king, the knight captures the queen for free! If the white king were not in check, and it were white's move here, where could the queen go to attack all three of black's pieces? Qd4+!

Be careful making a fork where you attack the same piece as yours. If that were a white knight on d2, the white knight would just capture the black knight. Look at Diagram 6.2 for an example of a strong double attack.

White's queen is aiming at the hanging rook and the pawn on h7. What happens if black saves the rook with . . . Rg8? Qxh7#!

What if black plays . . . Rb1+?

This is a good option! It's a forcing move. It loses the rook (Bxb1), but now black will be able to stop the mate (for a few moves). Another way to stop the immediate mate is to play Kg8, but of course white can simply take the rook (Qxb8+).

What if black moves the pawn to h6? Qxb8#.

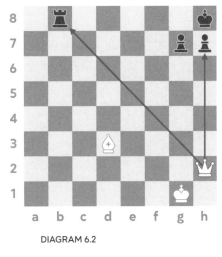

DIAGRAM 6.2

A STRONG DOUBLE ATTACK

In any case, white will win this game soon.

Forks and double attacks happen frequently in chess games, because every piece can create a fork. The queen and the knight are the best at making forks because they can both move in eight different directions!

Check it out!

Diagram 6.3 shows a common fork in the opening. How can white make a fork and win material? In other words, which move puts a white piece where it can attack two black pieces at once?

Play Nxf7, of course! You will be attacking the queen and the rook. Now look at Diagram 6.4.

Black will probably choose to save the queen, so you'll get the rook for free! Notice that the black king can't capture the knight on f7. The bishop on c4 is guarding the knight. That move would be illegal. Qe7 is really the only move for black here. Next white will play Nxh8!

DIAGRAM 6.3

Nxf7 WILL ATTACK THE QUEEN AND THE ROOK

DIAGRAM 6.4

WHITE TO PLAY Nxh8

DIAGRAM 6.5

QUIZ 1

Quiz 1. It's black's turn in Diagram 6.5. How can black create a fork in one move? This is from a real game played between Anthony Saidy and Bobby Fischer. Do you know about Bobby Fischer? He was a **chess prodigy** and the only **World Champion** from the United States!

Pin

This is my favorite tactic! That's probably because I love bishops and queens so much. Or maybe I love bishops and queens so much because I love pins! A pin makes something stay where it is.

There are two types of pins: an **absolute pin** and a **relative pin**. An absolute pin means the piece must absolutely stay there; it is illegal to move it. Therefore, you are pinning something to the king.

ABSOLUTE PIN:

If it were black's turn in Diagram 6.6, black would play . . . Qxh3#! The g2 pawn would love to try to capture the queen, but that would leave the white king in check, because of the bishop's position—so moving the pawn would be illegal. This means the bishop on b7 has pinned the pawn in place. Black just **exploited** the pin. Checkmate!

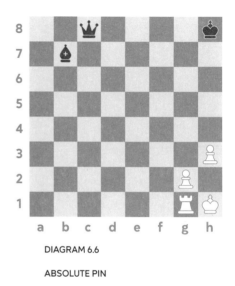

DIAGRAM 6.6

ABSOLUTE PIN

RELATIVE PIN:

Let's look carefully at the position in Diagram 6.7. The white rook on d1 is pinning the black knight on d5 to the black queen on d8. The knight is *allowed* to move, but it really shouldn't. If it were to capture the supposedly hanging bishop on b4, the rook would swoop forward and capture the queen! That would not be a good trade for black.

If it were white's turn here, they wouldn't actually capture the pinned piece. Do you see how they can create another pin? Bc4! This **puts pressure on the pinned piece** and also creates a **cross pin**. Now the

DIAGRAM 6.7

RELATIVE PIN

knight is absolutely pinned—if it captured the bishop or made any other move, the other bishop would be putting the king in danger. White will have two attackers on the knight and black has only one defender. White will capture the knight for free on the next turn.

What you should do if you have pinned your opponent:

- Capture the pinned piece (only if you win material and it's good for your position).
- Put pressure on the pinned piece.
- Exploit the pin (that means take advantage of the fact that the piece or pawn can't move).

What you should do if your opponent has pinned you:

- Get out of the pin.
- Break the pin with another piece.
- Look for **forcing moves.**

Check it out!

In Diagram 6.8, which is a real game played between two World Champions, how can black **exploit** the pin?

Former World Champion Viswanathan Anand (we call him Vishy, for short) just played move 30. Rf1. The player with black is the current World Chess Champion, Magnus Carlsen. He noticed that the rook on a2 is pinning the pawn on f2 to the square g2. Why is g2 important? If the pawn on f2 went missing, Qg2 would be mate! The white king would not be able to capture the black queen without being put in danger by the rook on a2.

So, black was able to exploit the pin with 30 . . . Rxe3! He is tempting the pawn on f2 to capture the rook. Of course, black shouldn't do it, and it's Vishy, so he doesn't fall for the mate in one. This game has a very exciting endgame. Take a look in the Resources section (see page 128) to discover where to find it and follow all the moves.

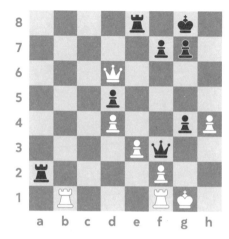

DIAGRAM 6.8

HOW CAN BLACK EXPLOIT THE PIN?

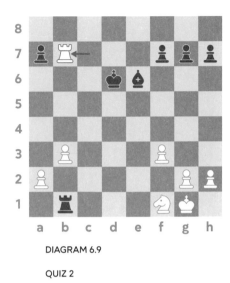

DIAGRAM 6.9

QUIZ 2

Quiz 2. Your turn! In the position in Diagram 6.9, seven-time US Champion GM Irina Krush (what a great name!) exploits one pin by putting pressure on another pinned piece. Krush has black against GM Camilla Baginskaite. What should black play?

PIN FACTS!

Only long-range pieces can create pins. (Do you remember which pieces can go long distances?)

→ There must be three pieces lined up to create a pin.
→ You'll need to **evaluate** and **calculate** what to do about the pin.
→ Pinning a piece is kind of like taking your opponent's piece and turning it into a chunk of concrete.
→ A pinned piece does not protect.

Skewer

This tactic is very similar to the pin. You will need to use a long-range piece; you will need three pieces lined up. The difference is that, in a pin, the more valuable piece is at one end and, in a skewer, the more valuable piece is in the middle (check back to part 1 to see how much each piece is worth). Some people call skewers X-rays because you see through the first piece to the piece behind it.

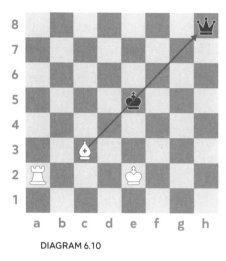

DIAGRAM 6.10

A SKEWER

Look at Diagram 6.10. The bishop skewers the king to the queen. The king is forced to move out of check, and the bishop will capture the queen. Black wishes he weren't in check here, so he could play Qh2+ and skewer the white king to the hanging rook on a2. Remember to always look for hanging pieces when evaluating the position.

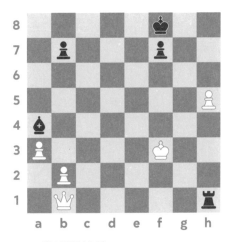

DIAGRAM 6.11

WHAT ARE THE QUEEN'S OPTIONS?

Check it out!

Diagram 6.11 shows an amazing position. It looks like the queen has a bunch of escape squares, or a hanging rook to capture. But everywhere she goes, she succumbs to a skewer or a pin! You may want to set this up on your own chessboard.

Let's look at the queen's options and their outcomes.

- Stay where she is: She'll be captured by the h1 rook.

- Move anywhere on the 1st rank: Same outcome.

- Qxh1: Bc6+ skewers the king to the queen.

- Qc2: The bishop just takes it!

- Qd3: Rh3+ skewer.

- Qe4: Bc6 pins the queen.

- Qf5: Rf1 skewer.

- Qg6: Pawn takes queen!

- Qh7 looks like it hides from tricks, but Rxh5! If Qxh5, she will be in a diagonal line with the king so Bd1+ skewers!

- Qa2 looks like it hides, but Bb3 threatens the queen and, if she takes him, Rh3+ will skewer the king to the queen that is now on b3!

Did you see all of that? Chess is patterns!

Quiz 3. You're going to use a combination! It's black's turn to move in Diagram 6.12. First, make a skewer (it's okay to give up a piece because you'll be able to win the queen). Then, after white moves, make a fork!

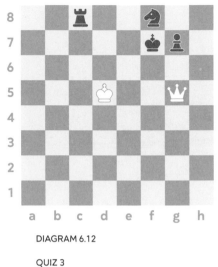

DIAGRAM 6.12

QUIZ 3

Discovered Attack

Don't you just love your long-range pieces so much now? Here is another tactic that uses the powers of the rook, bishop, and queen. Remember to look at the whole board when you're playing chess, and which pieces are on the same files, ranks, and diagonals as other pieces. Discovered attacks are the sneakiest of all. You may hear them called simply "discoveries" or "disco attacks."

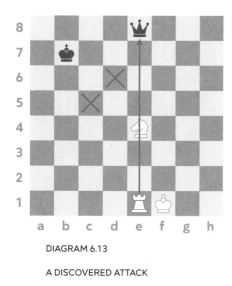

DIAGRAM 6.13

A DISCOVERED ATTACK

Look at Diagram 6.13. There are three pieces lined up (again). The piece in the middle moves and the piece behind it makes the attack! This tactic is a little harder because it's a two-parter: You need to see how to make the attack, then how to make the capture.

The knight moves and the queen is under attack *by the rook!* The rook is being kind of lazy, actually. He's like, "Hey, knight, scoot over. Okay, thanks. HI, QUEEN!" You could move the knight anywhere and the rook will attack the queen, but don't make random, hoping moves in chess. You should always look for forcing moves! Go forward and make check! It turns out there are two ways of doing this: Nd6+ is my favorite because it's also a fork—the knight will now be attacking both the king and queen! But Nc5+ also works. The queen can't block, so once the king gets out of check, you'll be able to capture the queen with your rook.

Take a look at the position in Diagram 6.14. Notice any differences? That's right, the king and queen are reversed. The supercool thing about the discovery is that it can be an attack on a king, too. We call this a **discovered check**. You can still move the knight to the same places, d6 or c5, to attack the queen, but one of the squares is better than the other.

It's d6 because that is more forcing. If Nc5+, the Queen could go to e7 (blocking the lazy rook's check) and even though you win the queen with the rook, the black king can take the rook back (did you see that?). With Nd6+ it's a fork, and also a **discovered double check**.

Whoa! Lots of tactics here. This time the queen can't block the check by the rook because the knight *also* gives check. Remember, you must always get your king out of danger! In a double check you can't block or capture (with another piece) to escape from check. You can only move your king! (Sometimes you can use your king to capture, but he must *always* move.) A discovered double check is the most forcing move in chess.

DIAGRAM 6.14

A DISCOVERED CHECK

Here is a great example of a discovered double check that leads to mate. The game is only 11 moves, and includes a great queen **sacrifice**. Follow along on your board! We are going to stop after move nine.

White	Black
Richard Réti	**Savielly Tartakower**
Vienna, Austria-Hungary, 1910	
1. e4	c6
2. d4	d5
3. Nc3	dxe4
4. Nxe4	Nf6
5. Qd3	e5
6. dxe5	Qa5+
7. Bd2	Qxe5
8. 0-0-0	Nxe4
9. Qd8+	Kxd8

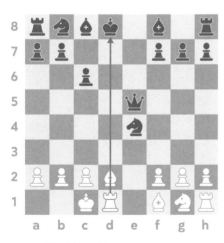

DIAGRAM 6.15

DISCOVERED DOUBLE CHECK

Your board should look like Diagram 6.15.

Do you see how the rook, bishop, and king are lined up? The bishop can make a discovered double check, and neither the queen nor knight could take it!

White	Black
10. Bg5++	Kc7
11. Bd8#	

If instead on move 10 . . . Ke8, it will still be mate with Rd8#. Helper mate!

Check it out!

Look at Diagram 6.16. I call this the **copycat opening**. It's not a good idea to copy *all* of your opponent's moves!

Where can the white knight go to make a discovered check that wins the queen?

If you chose Nc6+ you were correct! If you chose Nxf7+, look carefully at how black might escape from that check. Do you see how the king could

DIAGRAM 6.16

THE COPYCAT OPENING

DIAGRAM 6.17

QUIZ 4

simply take the knight and get out of check? With Nc6+, even though it looks like everyone in the world can capture that knight, *no piece can capture it*, because it's a discovered check by the queen on e2. The only thing black might try is Qe7 to block the check and try to tempt you to take it with your queen, when the bishop on c8 could take you back and trade. But nope! You'll snatch that queen up with your knight!

Quiz 4. White to move and make a discovered double check, then mate! Diagram 6.17 is a mate-in-two puzzle; I think you're ready for it.

The Sacrifice

A sacrifice is when you give something up to get something better. This is a crucial tactic that you must be willing to do when you play.

For example, what's better than a queen? Checkmate! Look at Diagram 6.18 for an example.

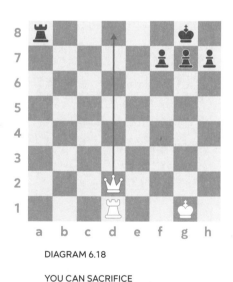

DIAGRAM 6.18

YOU CAN SACRIFICE
THE QUEEN HERE

White	Black
1. Qd8+!	Rxd8
2. Rxd8#	

You can give away your queen in Diagram 6.18 because she is in a battery with the rook. The rook backs up the queen. Even though you "lose" 9 points at first, you get checkmate, which always wins!

Check it out!

Now look at Diagram 6.19. You can "sac" your queen again with Qg8+!

After the rook captures the queen (Rxg8), you can make checkmate. Look at Diagram 6.20. Do you see how?

Don't capture the rook back! Nf7#!

That's called a *smothered mate*. The king is trapped by his own pieces.

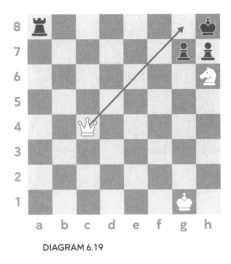

DIAGRAM 6.19

"SAC" YOUR QUEEN

DIAGRAM 6.20

A SMOTHERED MATE

DIAGRAM 6.21

QUIZ 5

DIAGRAM 6.22

QUIZ 6

Quiz 5. You try it! White to move.

Can you find a forcing move for white in Diagram 6.21? It won't matter how black responds, it will be game over in two moves!

Diagram 6.22 shows a fantastic game with two amazing sacrifices played by five-time (and current at the time this book was written) US Champion Hikaru Nakamura. He is black against strong GM Boris Gelfand from Israel. At the time they played this game, Gelfand was **rated** higher!

Note: You are looking at this match from black's point of view—you can always check the letters and numbers along the edges to make sure.

Quiz 6. Black played Nxe1 here. What if white plays cxd8=Q? I mean, white would have TWO queens!

Quiz 7. A few moves later (Diagram 6.23), Nakamura (black) sacs his queen! What if white takes it with his f1 bishop?

BLITZ CHESS

Nakamura is one of the fastest players in the world. In 2014 he was ranked #1 in the world for "blitz" chess. That's when, for your whole game, you only get five minutes to play! (Your opponent has five minutes as well. Whoever loses on time first, loses the game!) He is also amazing at a game called "bullet" chess. You both only get ONE minute to play your entire game! I don't recommend it because you can't really think in that amount of time, but Nakamura has great intuition. He wrote a book called *Bullet Chess: One Minute to Mate.*

DIAGRAM 6.23

QUIZ 7

Remove the Guard, Decoy, Deflection

This tactic may also be called remove the defender. Sometimes you'd like to get into the king's castle and do some damage, but asking politely just won't do—the guard is having none of it.

What do you do? You resort to tactics: Get rid of the guard! There are different ways to go about it.

In Diagram 6.24, white would like to take the bishop, but it's guarded by the knight. Remove the guard by capturing it!

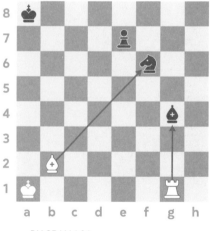

DIAGRAM 6.24

REMOVE THE GUARD

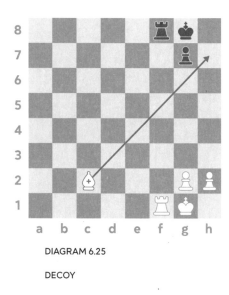

DIAGRAM 6.25

DECOY

White	Black
1. Bxf6	exf6
2. Rxg4	

Almost any other bishop move by black would have led to 2. Bxe7 and white would have won a knight and a pawn for free.

Another way to remove the defender is to decoy the guard away. Lure it with something tempting. Want a hanging piece? Look at Diagram 6.25.

You could have just traded rooks, right? But even better is removing the defender (the king) by decoying him away from the rook. If you move your bishop to h7, the black king will have to capture the bishop (or move to h8). Then you can capture the rook, and you'll have won material!

Diagram 6.26 shows GM Hou Yifan from China, the current highest-rated woman chess player in the world (and former Women's World Champion), using this tactic in her game against the Bulgarian GM, Antoaneta Stefanova, a former Women's

DIAGRAM 6.26

YIFAN VS. STEFANOVA

World Champion. This game was played during the Women's Grand Prix in 2014.

Black just played . . . Rc8. Yes, you could just trade rooks, but let's look a little deeper. Who is guarding the rook? Can we force her to move away? Remove the guard by moving your pawn to g4! Even though black can capture it (. . . hxg4), white can capture again (with the other pawn, hxg4!). Now the queen is under attack. The pawn on g4 is protected by the white queen. Do you see anywhere safe for the black queen to go, so she still guards the rook? (Hint: The answer is no.)

Check it out!

Sometimes you have to play **fantasy chess.** You see a checkmate pattern; you make a plan to make it happen! Look at Diagram 6.27. This is Fischer versus Sanchez in 1959.

White wants to play Re7#, but the black bishop on b4 guards that square. Fischer played Bd2 to

DIAGRAM 6.27

FISCHER VS. SANCHEZ

decoy it! If . . . Bxd2 then the rook can easily slide over to e7. The king can't capture it because it's guarded by the knight, and the black bishop is too far away on d2 to capture the rook either. The king can't escape to d5 because of the pawn on e4. Mate! See how this works?

Quiz 8. Your turn! In this quiz (Diagram 6.28), if it's white's turn, you'll use a deflection. It's like a decoy sacrifice. White can see a fantasy back rank checkmate, but the rook on d7 is in the way. Deflect him away, even if you have to sacrifice your queen! Look for forcing checks.

The cool thing about this puzzle is it can also work if it's black's turn. Remember to look for elements of the puzzle. Fantasy chess: Black would love to create a semi-smothered mate with the knight on h2. The white queen guards that square. Deflect the queen with a sacrifice. Mate!

Removing the guard requires that you *think several moves ahead*. We will practice this more in chapter 7.

DIAGRAM 6.28

QUIZ 8

HOW TO PLAY CHESS FOR KIDS

CHECKMATE!

• •

Here is what you learned in chapter 6:

☑ Forks, or double attacks, are where one piece attacks two things.

☑ Pins make something stay where it is. You can exploit that piece!

☑ Skewers are similar to pins but the more valuable piece is in the middle.

☑ Discovered attacks happen when the piece in the middle moves and the piece behind it makes the attack.

☑ Double checks are a type of discovered check and are the most forcing moves in chess.

☑ Sacrifices occur when you give something up to get something better.

☑ Removing the guard eliminates a defender so you can get what you want.

☑ You can capture the guard, decoy it away, or deflect it to a different square.

7 SUPER STRATEGIES

In this chapter you will learn strategies to get a strong position. A good position leads to tactics! Strategies in general have to do with pawn structure, where to place your pieces so they have the most freedom and attacking possibilities, and king safety. They are different from tactics in that they are more about the position and long term. Tactics are quick tricks to win material or the game; strategies are ways to get you there. We will talk about controlling the board, planning, thinking ahead, and what happens if you don't castle. Finally, I will show you a way to beat your parents and your friends in only four moves!

Control the Board

In chess, as in boxing, fencing, soccer, or most competitive sports, you will have to take the **initiative** and attack if you want to win. Playing defense is required *sometimes*, but if you start out playing defensively, you can't win. Remember to have confidence! Try stuff! You will win some and lose some, but you won't learn unless you try.

In the beginning of the game it is critical to control the center of the board. In part 1 we identified the four center squares (d4, d5, e4, and e5). In the opening you want to put your pawns and pieces in the center, or attacking the center. In the middle game, you have three places you can attack: the kingside, the queenside, or the center. You will attack where you have a strength and your opponent has a weakness.

Vera Menchik won the first Women's World Chess Championship in 1927 and continued to win until her untimely death in 1944. There are lots of interesting facts about Menchik—for example, why would Max Euwe, the

DIAGRAM 7.1

MENCHIK VS. GRAF

fifth World Chess Champion, be in the Menchik Club? Look her up!

Diagram 7.1 shows a game against her rival Sonja Graf in 1937. Menchik has already developed her pieces toward the center. Where should she attack? Let's evaluate the position.

Material is even. Remember that material means pieces. So, both sides have the same pieces. Both of white's bishops are aiming at the kingside. The white queen has lots of freedom. The black bishop on c8 is undeveloped and the rooks are not **connected** (able to guard each other along their first rank). Either side could take control over the open d file. Both sides are castled, but whose king seems weaker?

Menchik (white) has decided to play 17. Ng5 to attack the kingside! Follow along on your board to see what happens.

White	Black
Vera Menchik	**Sonja Graf**
Vienna, Austria-Hungary, 1937	
17. Ng5	g6
18. Qf3 (continuing to bring pieces to the king-side and threatening the hanging rook)	Bb7 (This is a strategy called *fianchetto*—you put the bishop in the little cave where the pawns surround it, and it attacks the center from the side. Here it attacks the queen.)
19. Qh3 (saving the queen and bringing it closer to the attack)	h5
20. Rd1 (Notice how white uses all her pieces?)	Ng4
21. Rd7 (Sacking the rook! And black resigned in light of . . .)	Qxd7
22. Qxh5 (A queen sacrifice!)	gxh5
23. Bh7# (One white bishop is attacking the king, and the other is pointed at both of his possible escape squares—checkmate!)	

DIAGRAM 7.2

MENCHIK VS. GRAF
CONTINUED

DIAGRAM 7.3

KASPAROV VS. X3D FRITZ

DIAGRAM 7.4

KASPAROV VS. X3D FRITZ
CONTINUED

Check it out!

You don't always attack on the kingside. Look at Diagram 7.3. In this game between former World Champion Garry Kasparov and the computer X3D Fritz (in the Man versus Machine World Chess Championship), how can you control the board on the queenside?

Kasparov was the highest ranked player in the world for 225 out of 228 months (19 years). He noticed his **river of pawns** was headed toward the queen's side of the board. The "river of pawns" refers to the incredible pawn chain: f2, e3, d4, c5! How can you make the chain even longer?

By playing b4 (headed to b6)! Diagram 7.4 shows the game a little later, after white brings all his pieces to the queenside.

Wow! Kasparov was able to win this game due to his complete control over the queenside. Black ran out of good moves.

Use All Your Pieces

This is critical if you want to win! You can't win just by dancing your knight around the board.

It is important to harmonize your pieces and make a plan. Don't just develop randomly. Make sure each move has a purpose. In general, you want to develop your center pawns, your knights toward the center, and your bishops after that. Remember CDC from the section on openings. Look at Diagram 7.5 and watch how Magnus Carlsen, at 16 years old, developed all his pieces to help him attack the center of the board. Diagram 7.5 is from the 2007 game in which he beat the **FIDE** (that's the World Chess Organization) World Champion from Bulgaria, Veselin Topalov.

All of white's pieces are set up aiming at the center of the board. They are perfectly poised to continue a plan to attack the middle of the board! Carlsen played e4 next and, eventually, won on move 64.

DIAGRAM 7.5

CARLSEN VS. TOPALOV

DIAGRAM 7.6

MORPHY VS. MARACHE

DIAGRAM 7.7

MORPHY VS. MARACHE
CONTINUED

Check it out!

Paul Morphy, the first unofficial World Champion around 1858, was known for developing, castling, sacrificing, and winning. He almost always coordinated all his pieces. Morphy's games are very instructive. I would look them up if I were you. Check out the Resources section (page 128) for where to find great games like these.

Look at Diagram 7.6. Morphy is black against Napoleon Marache in 1857. (That's a long time ago—good thing they notated!) Let's look at black's pieces. The queen is pinning the pawn on g2. The knights are guarding each other and ready to attack the kingside. The bishop on a5 is guarding the pawn on c3, which is preventing white's knight from developing! His rook is on an open file and his king has castled. Great positions equal great tactics! Black played Ng3 in Diagram 7.7, completely winning. If anything takes the knight, bye-bye, queen (. . . Qxe4)! White played Qxg6, but this loses to Nde2# (that means the knight that was on d went to e2, not the knight from g3).

Look at Diagram 7.8. How would you use all your pieces in this position to continue a plan? My hero, the Hungarian GM Judit Polgár, who broke Bobby Fischer's record as youngest Grandmaster and was the top-rated woman chess player in the world for 26 years, has white in this game versus GM Alexei Shirov in 1995. First, develop with a forcing move. Then develop again with another forcing move! This leads to an awesome tactic.

Look at Diagram 7.9. White played Bg5+. Black then played . . . Ndf6. White's next move was Rd1, attacking the queen, skewering it to the square d7, and when black retreated his queen to b7, Polgár raced her rook down the open file to d7. That's check, forking the queen and king, and the knight on f6 is pinned by the bishop white put on g5!

Shirov resigned two moves later. If you resign, you give up and automatically lose. I don't recommend resigning until you're a professional, because we all

DIAGRAM 7.8

POLGAR VS. SHIROV

DIAGRAM 7.9

POLGAR VS. SHIROV CONTINUED

make mistakes! You could get a stalemate or other type of draw, but you don't give yourself that chance if you give up.

If you use all your pieces in an attack, you are more likely to be successful. Try not to leave anyone behind. When I'm not sure what to do, I try to get my pieces to better squares. Pieces love to work together to attack specific parts of the board.

EVERYONE MAKES MISTAKES

As you are starting out, don't assume anything! Look at Diagram 7.10. In 1902, Georg Marco, with black, versus Ignatz von Popiel, assumed he was going to lose his bishop on d4. He resigned. He could instead have played Bg1 with a discovered attack on the queen by the rook on d7, and another attack on h2. If white played Qxd7, Marco could have taken h2 with his queen—mate!

DIAGRAM 7.10
MARCO VS.
POPIEL

HOW TO PLAY CHESS FOR KIDS

Think Ahead

You often hear that chess players can think many moves ahead. The first step to doing this is seeing ONE move ahead. Does that sound silly? Well, believe it or not, that is the quickest way to win as you improve your other tactics and strategies.

You'll ask yourself, before placing a piece down, "If I go here, will it be hanging or protected?" And you'll ask the same for your opponent's moves.

Once you've got that down (it will take you a while, but you'll get it—play slowly), you'll start to **calculate**. This strategy requires that you think about what your opponent will play if you play a certain move. You'll be considering their best moves—don't assume they will play badly! We often talk about **candidate moves** in chess. This means you should consider three possible moves each turn. It becomes a kind of tree. Imagine you think of a move, then you think of your opponent's response to that move, and you think of your response to that. Then you go back to the beginning and think of a second candidate move, and follow the same process.

GM Maurice Ashley was the first black grandmaster; he is a Jamaican American player who often is invited to be a commentator at prestigious chess tournaments. I met him when I lived in Brooklyn. He was giving a free lecture to neighborhood schoolkids, and I was teaching chess at a public school at the time. I was lucky to be able to meet him—he is a really cool guy!

Look at Diagram 7.11. He has white against GM Boris Kreiman in this game in 1992. He noticed the diagonal to black's king was easily opened and found an amazing tactic.

Set this position up on your board!

DIAGRAM 7.11

ASHLEY VS. KREIMAN

White	Black
Maurice Ashley	**Boris Kreiman**
29. Nxf6	Qxd3 (Queen sacrifice!)
30. Re8+ (forcing check)	Bf8
31. Rxf8+ (He just takes it.)	Kg7
32. Nd7+	

DIAGRAM 7.12

ASHLEY VS. KREIMAN CONTINUED

Then black resigned, because if the black king moved to g6, the white knight could go to e5 and fork the king and queen. See Diagram 7.12. White is clearly winning.

Ashley had to see all those moves ahead, though, before he could give up his queen. When you look for candidate moves, always consider forcing moves. Forcing moves are checks, threats, and captures.

Quiz 1. Try to think through the next three moves for black in Diagram 7.13. White, GM Nana Dzagnidze, has just promoted a pawn to a queen. Black is the 20-year-old GM Aleksandra Goryachkina. This game is from the Women's Candidate Tournament in 2019.

DIAGRAM 7.13

QUIZ 1

Castle Early

Remember when we learned about castling, way back in part 1? The king moves two squares toward a rook, and that rook jumps over and lands right next to the king. I said that all professionals castle, and I suggest castling within the first 10 moves as you are starting your chess career. (When you are a professional, you get to decide when to break the rules.) Here's what can happen if you don't castle.

Check it out!

DIAGRAM 7.14

SHIROV VS. LAPINSKI

Look at Diagram 7.14. It's Shirov again, on the winning side this time. He's playing white against Lapinski in 1990.

The classic sacrifice on f7, the weakest square on the board, lures the king out. No castling allowed now, because the king will have moved! Set this one up. It's a **miniature**. A miniature is a game that lasts fewer than 20 moves.

White	Black
Alexei Shirov	**Jerzy Lapinksi**
8. Bf7+	Kxf7
9. d4 (discovered attack on the pinned pawn on f4)	Qxd4+
10. Be3 (The pawn can't capture because it's pinned, protecting its king from the white queen!)	Qf6
11. Bxf4	Ke8
12. Nc3 (develops the knight to the happy square)	Nc6
13. Nd5	Qg6
14. Rae1+ (continues to develop with **tempo**)	Be7
15. Bd6	

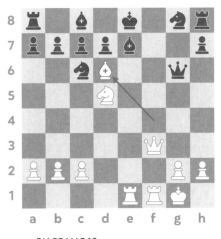

DIAGRAM 7.15

SHIROV VS. LAPINSKI POSITION AFTER MOVE 15. Bd6

Look at Diagram 7.15. The black bishop can't take because it's pinned, protecting its king from the white rook on e1. And if the queen or pawn captures the bishop, Qf8 is mate!

...	Kd8
16. Qf8+	Bxf8
17. Bxc7#	

DIAGRAM 7.16

SHIROV VS. LAPINSKI POSITION
AFTER 17. Bxc7#

DIAGRAM 7.17

QUIZ 2

Now see Diagram 7.16. The final position looks like this. White developed, used his pieces harmoniously, castled, sacrificed, pinned, put pressure on the pinned piece, made a discovered attack, put his rooks on open files, looked for forcing moves, made a plan to attack the king, and calculated candidate moves! (See? Easy.)

Quiz 2. In Diagram 7.17, white is to move and make checkmate in one move.

Go for a Quick Checkmate

There is a trick in chess that every student must learn: It's called the *scholar's mate*, or the four-move mate. Scholar means student—many students try this checkmate. It won't work every time, but it sure is fun when it does! This happened to me in real life, when I was in high school. I was on the top board for my team, in a room of 100 players. It was silent, and the games had just begun. Thirty seconds later, my opponent loudly called out, "Checkmate!" I was mortified! I felt all the eyes in the room turn toward me. It was the last time I ever lost because of this four-move mate.

Now that we know that f7 is the weakest square on the board, we can see how to achieve this checkmate!

There are different ways of going about it, but I like placing the queen on h5 on move 2 because it also attacks the hanging pawn on e5. We are attacking f7 once, but it is defended once by the king. Look at Diagram 7.18. How can we bring out a helper?

The bishop on the white square! Notice how f7 is a white square? We'll need our white-square bishop to help out.

Assuming black protects the e pawn with something like Nc6, you can play Bc4. Here is where black has to pay attention! If black is not focused, it's lights out!

DIAGRAM 7.18

THE QUEEN IMMEDIATELY ATTACKS THE HANGING PAWN ON e5

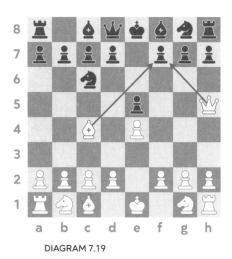

DIAGRAM 7.19

TWO ATTACKERS AND ONE
DEFENDER ON f7

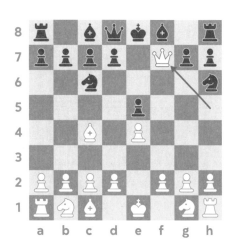

DIAGRAM 7.20

DON'T PLAY 4. Qxf7+ HERE
DUE TO 4 . . . Nxf7!

Look at Diagram 7.19. There are two attackers and one defender on f7. If black plays Nf6 or a similar move, Qxf7 is mate! (Not Bxf7, which allows the king to escape to e7.)

Here are the moves:

White	Black
1. e4	e5
2. Qh5	Nc6
3. Bc4	Nf6
4. Qxf7#	

Instead of 3 . . . Nf6, it would be better for black to try 3 . . . Qe7 or 3 . . . Qf6 to guard f7 again. Some kids try the sneaky move, 3 . . . Nh6.

White gets very excited and plants the queen on f7. But is it mate? Nope. 4 . . . Nxf7 and white loses the queen. See Diagram 7.20.

That's the *scholar's mate*. Now go beat your parents and friends!

CHECKMATE!

∙∙

Here's what you learned in chapter 7:

☑ Control the board by taking initiative and finding a weakness to attack.

☑ Use all your pieces; don't leave anyone out at the party. Be nice to your pieces.

☑ Make a plan! Don't just put pieces on random squares (we call that pushing wood).

☑ Think ahead; calculate three candidate moves. What happens next?

☑ If you don't castle early, your king could get into trouble, especially on f7.

☑ The four-move mate is fun—if you are on the winning side!

8 MOVING ON

In this chapter, I will give you ideas on continuing your chess education and beginning to compete. You've learned so much already! There are levels to everything, and you have to keep playing to improve and get to the next level.

Keep Playing

If you've gotten this far, you have completed a basic training course in chess. You are ready to compete and win! To get better, though, you have to practice. Put your skills to use! You know how all the pieces move, their strengths and values; you know tactics and strategies. There are many ways to practice. You can check out the Resources section (page 128) to find websites, books, and apps where you can practice your tactics. You can play online, of course. But the best way to improve is simply to play against another person in real life.

Reach Out and Compete

How can you play more chess? Here are some ideas. Play your little brother. Play your parents and grandparents. Play against yourself—you will always win.

You could also join a chess club at your school. There may or may not be a chess coach, but there should be an adult there who can help you. If there isn't a chess club at your school, start one! My mom helped me start a club at my middle school. Lots of kids wanted to join!

Look at the United States Chess Federation (USCF) website for national events. Often there are no qualifying events beforehand, and you can just play without being specifically invited. For USCF tournaments, you'll need a membership. I suggest getting the one with a monthly magazine for kids!

Each state typically has their own chess organization with a calendar of events that will often list chess clubs in different cities. Maybe there is one in your neighborhood! Some clubs are just for adults, and some are just for kids, and some are for any skill level, kid or adult. I recommend checking out a club's website or calling the club to find out more. And you can totally play against adults. That's pretty much all I did when I was a kid. It's excellent practice—and they are always surprised when you beat them!

You can enter any tournament that has an "under" section. "Under" refers to a rating cap. So, if your rating is 100, you would want to play in an under-500 section. If your rating is 800, you would play in an under 1000. Different tournaments have different under sections. You will start out unrated, but once you have your membership, you'll get a rating after 25 games. That number *sort of* reflects how strong you are at chess. But don't get obsessed with it—it's just a number! It will fluctuate a lot as you start out. Sometimes there are unrated tournaments; I run tournaments that have rated and unrated sections. If you can find a tournament with unrated sections, it might be a good place to begin, as there will be less pressure.

You can always get a private chess coach. But play a whole bunch first. It's not necessary to have a coach right away.

When you're looking for apps and online chess sites, a good bet is to go for ones with the word "kid" in their names. Those will be designed just for you! Not too easy, not too hard. Check out the Resources section (page 128) for a few options.

CHECKMATE!

· ·

Here's what you learned in chapter 8:

☑ You are a genius for reading this entire book!

☑ Now you need to practice.

☑ You can play anyone at chess, in any country, at any age, as long as they know how to play!

☑ There might be a chess club at your school or in your city.

☑ Try out a tournament—the unrated section is a good place to start.

☑ Get your USCF membership at uschess.org.

☑ Practice your skills online and on your electronic devices.

QUIZ ANSWERS

CHAPTER THREE

Quiz 1: Move the rook to h1: *Anastasia's mate.* The knight is attacking the empty escape squares, the king can't take his own pawn, and the rook puts the king in check while guarding the entire h file. Black cannot move, block, or capture.

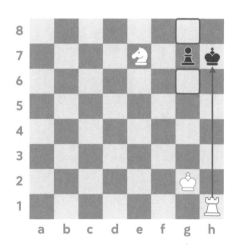

Quiz 2: Move the bishop to g3: *Boden's mate* (also called *crisscross mate*). The bishop is checking the king, and the queen guards all the escape squares.

Quiz 3: Capture the pawn on f7 with your knight: *smothered mate!*

Quiz 4: The queen goes to a8 for mate: *back rank mate*. The queen puts the king in danger and guards the 8th rank, whereas the rook on f1 prevents the king from running away. There is no way to block or capture.

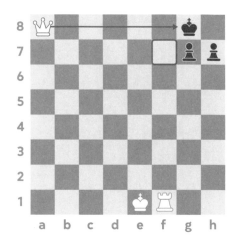

CHAPTER FOUR

The five checkmating moves are queen to d1, e1, f1 = *back rank mate*. Queen to g2 or h2 = *helper mate*. (Or a *queen sandwich*. As long as your king is helping protect the queen, that's the most important!)

CHAPTER SIX

Quiz 1: Qe1+ forks the king and the hanging rook on a5.

Quiz 2: . . . Bc4! This puts pressure on the absolutely pinned knight on f1 and also exploits the relative pin the black rook has (on the b3 pawn to the rook on b7). Did you see both of those pins?

If white uses its b3 pawn to capture the bishop with bxc4, then black can capture the white rook with . . . Rxb7: bye-bye, rookie! Black is attacking the knight twice—with the bishop and the rook—and it's defended only once (by the king). Krush captured the knight safely on her next turn. (If she were to capture the knight first, she would lose 2 points and, eventually, the game. Do you see why? The king would simply capture the rook back!)

Quiz 3: Black plays Rc5+, skewering the king to the queen. Once the king takes the rook, Ne6+ forks the king and the queen! White will need to move the king out of check and lose the queen on his next turn.

Quiz 4: Nf6++ forces the king into the corner. The bishop can't take the knight because of the discovered check by the queen. After Kh8, Qh7 is mate. The king can't take the queen because the knight is in position to check it—that would be illegal. Checkmate, good game!

Quiz 5: Answer: 1. Qxf7+

If black's king runs into the corner (1 . . . Kh8), then:

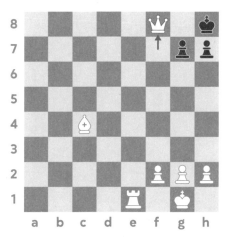

we take the rook! 2. Qxf8#. Back rank mate!

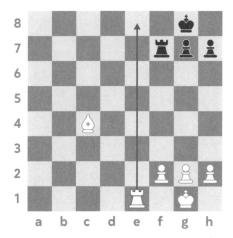

If instead the rook takes the queen on f7 (1 . . . Rxf7),

then we play 2. Re8#. Back rank mate! See how the rook

on f7 is pinned by the bishop on c4? It can't move to the 8th rank to protect the king, because that would mean black is putting himself in check by the bishop. You have combined a sacrifice with a pin! Sacrifices often work in conjunction with other tactics. That's called a **combination**.

Quiz 6: . . . g2 is mate! Two queens won't stop black's pawn from attacking the king.

Quiz 7: . . . Bg2 is mate! With that bishop on d3, black's h3 bishop is free to get in position to attack the king.

Quiz 8: Answer for white: 1. Qxc7+ Rxc7; 2. Rd8+ Rc8; 3. (either rook) Rxc8#: You just solved a mate-in-three! Answer for black: 1 . . . Qxf2+; 2. Qxf2 Nxh2#.

CHAPTER SEVEN

Quiz 1: . . . Qd1+ forces the king to the c file. Then . . . Qc1+ skewers the king to the queen. When the king moves, Qxc8! The newly promoted queen doesn't even get a chance to move.

Quiz 2: Qxf7#

RESOURCES

Websites

365chess.com helps you learn about chess openings by searching through famous games.

Chessbase.com has current chess news, tournaments, and other cool information.

Chessgames.com provides 918,000 famous games you can research and review.

Chesskid.com offers amazing videos, lessons, puzzles, and articles—and you can play kids from around the world! (Plus, take a peek at the "Authors" section, and you'll see I've written hundreds of articles for them!)

USchess.org, the website of the United States Chess Federation, supplies information about upcoming tournaments and lists local clubs where you can learn more about what's happening near you. Plus, you can get a USCF membership and a rating, and then you can play in any tournament in the United States!

Books

Any *Chess Camp* book by Igor Sukhin will help you. There are five books in this set, and you can work through them as you would a workbook. They get progressively more difficult. The puzzles are thematic and really help you solidify the information.

Any workbook by Jeff Coakley is good. Here you can practice your tactics and strategies in puzzles and brief lessons. The green book is my favorite.

Bobby Fischer's Outrageous Chess Moves, by Bruce Pandolfini, is a great resource. I love this book! It starts out with positions from Fischer's games and you have to discover the best move. Below each puzzle is a clue, the answer, and an explanation. At the back of the book, Pandolfini provides each of the games from which he took the positions, so you can see how Fischer reached that position!

Chess Openings: Traps and Zaps, by Bruce Pandolfini, will teach you new tricks in the opening! Pandolfini has written a ton of great books.

In *How to Beat Your Dad at Chess*, Murray Chandler describes basic checkmates, as well as more difficult ones, that you can learn in a step-by-step process.

Learning Chess Manual for Chess Trainers, by Rob Brunia and Cor van Wijgerden, is not just for trainers—kids can use it, too (I recommend Step 1 and Step 2). For younger children, I recommend that a parent help them work through the book. It is structured as lessons, with puzzles included to see how well you've learned each theme!

Logical Chess: Move by Move by Irving Chernev is a fascinating book. If you want to know why the Grandmasters make their moves, this book explains *every single move!* It is extremely useful and insightful to see how GMs think.

My First Chess Book: 35 Easy and Fun Chess Activities for Children Aged 7+ is a book by Jessica (Martin) Prescott. That's me! This book is nontraditional in that it is a book of activities. You can set up positions with a few pieces (or all of them), and play different variations of chess to help you practice specific strategies and tactics. There are games like Bughouse, Ghost Chess, and Take Me, each of which helps you practice specific skills. You can play with a friend or family member, or even by yourself!

Play Like a Girl!, by Jennifer Shahade, is focused on female chess players. Women are underrepresented in the chess world. This book highlights some major female chess players and provides many thematic puzzles.

The Chess Kid's Book of Checkmate is one of my favorites by David MacEnulty, because, in it, he breaks the mates down into patterns.

Apps

Chess (from Chess.com, a little harder than Chesskid)

Chess Clock (time your games!)

Chesskid (my all-time favorite, hands-down—play, learn, have fun)

Chess King (multiple options, from openings, tactics, and strategies to checkmates—a little more advanced)

Play Magnus (play the World Champion at different ages in his life!)

Tactic Trainer (a bit trickier puzzle solving)

Make sure you have fun with chess! If one resource doesn't work for you, go to the next. There are lots of ways to study chess, and the best way to improve is to play!

GLOSSARY

50-MOVE RULE: This is a way to claim a draw—after 50 moves have passed without a capture or a pawn move. If you move a pawn on the 49th move, you have to start counting at one again. This does not occur in the opening because you are moving pawns and capturing things all the time. It generally occurs when someone doesn't know how to win, and they just chase the king all over the board without making any progress.

ABSOLUTE PIN: This occurs when a piece is unable to move because, if it did, the king would be in danger.

ACTIVE: This means a piece is participating in the game and doing a job.

BACK RANK MATE: This is one of the most common ways of making checkmate. The king is trapped on the back rank of the chessboard in checkmate. He can't move forward at all.

BASE OF THE PAWN CHAIN: The weakest part of the pawn chain is the base—the one at the bottom of the chain—because no one guards that pawn.

BATTERY: A battery is formed when two long-range pieces work together in the same file, rank, or diagonal.

CALCULATE: This is to visualize, or use your mind's eye, to see what could happen next—or even further ahead in the game—based on your moves and strategy.

CANDIDATE MOVES: These are choices you calculate before actually deciding on a move. Try to come up with three candidate moves before actually taking your turn. This takes patience and practice!

CASTLING: This special move protects your king. The king moves two squares toward the rook, and the rook jumps over the king and lands right next to him.

CHAIN: Pawns can protect each other when they are in a diagonal. One pawn will protect the one in front of it, diagonally. It's like they are holding hands.

CHECK: The king is in danger! You must move, block, or capture to escape from danger, if you can.

CHECKMATE: If you cannot move, block, or capture to escape from check, you're in checkmate. Game over!

CHESS PRODIGY: A young person who is an incredibly strong player and who seems to have picked up the game naturally is considered a prodigy. These players are unusual. Most of us have to learn the hard way and put in the work to be good. By the way, chess prodigies start out good but, to get better, they work hard, too!

CLOSED POSITION: Pawns locked up in the center of the board.

COMBINATION: Two or more tactics in a row constitute a combination, or combo.

CROSS PIN: Another pin, created in a different direction, but that is still aiming at the same pinned piece.

DEVELOPMENT: Moving pieces toward the center of the board, usually in the opening.

DISCOVERED ATTACK: With three pieces lined up, when the middle piece moves, the piece behind it makes an attack.

DISCOVERED CHECK: With three pieces lined up, when the middle piece moves, the piece behind it makes a check.

DISCOVERED DOUBLE CHECK: With three pieces lined up, the middle piece moves, and now both that piece and the piece behind it give check.

DOUBLE ATTACK: One piece attacks two of the opponent's pieces or a piece and a square.

DOUBLE CHECK: Two pieces giving check at the same time.

DRAW: This is a tied game: no one wins and no one loses. There are seven different ways of making a draw.

EN PASSANT: This special move allows one pawn to capture another if it has passed over the first pawn's original capture square. The pawns must be side by side, and you have to make the capture immediately if you choose to do it, or you will lose your chance with those particular pawns.

ENDGAME: When most of the pieces have come off the board, you have reached an endgame. Sometimes, even if there are still several pieces on the board, but the queens have been traded off, it is still called an endgame.

EVALUATE: This means you figure certain things out—who has more material, how safe each king is, which pieces are attacking which squares, and what the pawn structure looks like—before thinking of candidate moves.

EXPLOIT: This is what you can do to a pin. You take advantage of the fact that the piece or pawn cannot, or should not, move.

FANTASY CHESS: You imagine the best position, often a checkmate, and then you try to make a plan to achieve this fantasy.

FIANCHETTO (PRONOUNCED "FEE-AN-KETTO"): The bishop is developed onto the longest diagonal on the board. You can achieve this by moving the knight's pawn up one square, creating an upside-down V with your pawns. The bishop goes in that little cave and attacks the center from the side.

FIDE: Fédération Internationale des Échecs, or World Chess Federation

FILE: A vertical line on the chessboard, defined by letters. For example, the a file describes all the squares in a line on the left-hand side of the board, when you are playing with white pieces.

FORCING MOVES: Forcing moves are checks, threats, or captures. These are moves that limit the opponent's options.

FORK: When one piece attacks two pieces (the knight and queen are the best at creating forks).

GRANDMASTER (GM): GMs have reached the highest level of chess players and have ratings above 2500.

HANGING: An unprotected piece that can be captured for free.

HELPER MATE: When one piece puts the king in check and is right up next to the king, the other helps by protecting that piece so the king cannot capture it.

HOPING MOVES: The opposite of a forcing move is a hoping move. Don't assume your opponent will make a bad move. Always play the best moves!

HORWITZ BISHOPS: Bernard Horwitz was a German chess master who played in the nineteenth century. He discovered that bishops on adjacent diagonals were very powerful, as they controlled both black and white squares.

ILLEGAL: A move that is not allowed in chess. If either player makes an illegal move, do not continue—rewind and try again.

INITIATIVE: Taking initiative is starting the attack—an important element of winning.

KINGSIDE: This is the king's side of the board, if you divide the board vertically.

LADDER MATE: Also called a back rank mate, this is when the king is trapped on the edge of the board and two rooks (or two queens, or a queen and a rook) are guarding both ranks, checking the king, and preventing him from coming forward to the next rank. Checkmate!

LONG-RANGE PIECES: These pieces can go long distances in chess. Only the rook, queen, and bishop are long-range pieces.

MATERIAL: Pieces and pawns.

MATING MATERIAL: The pieces you need to force a checkmate. In the endgame, you need to have either a queen, one or two rooks, or two bishops to force a checkmate, if those are the only pieces on the board. A pawn can be considered mating material if it can be promoted. (You can make checkmate with a bishop and knight, but it's superhard, so don't worry if you just call that a draw.)

MIDDLE GAME: The part of the game after one or both sides have castled and most knights and bishops have been developed.

MINIATURE: A game that finishes in fewer than 20 moves.

NOTATION: Taking notation means you are writing down all of the moves in a game. You can review your game when you're done!

OPENING: The beginning of a chess game, when you start to develop your pieces.

OPPONENT: The person you are playing against.

PASSED PAWN: No pawn can stop yours from promoting—there is no pawn on your pawn's file, nor to the right or left files. It can't be captured by a pawn. Push passed pawns!

PIN: This makes a piece stay where it is. It's either a bad idea or illegal to move a pinned piece.

POSITION: The structure of the pieces and pawns on the board.

PROMOTION: When a pawn reaches the other side of the board, it may transform into a queen, rook, bishop, or knight. Most people choose a queen.

PUT PRESSURE ON THE PINNED PIECE: Attack the pinned piece again!

QUEEN DANCE: A very important technique to know when you have one queen left versus a lone king. Your king and queen work together to create checkmate.

QUEENSIDE: The queen's side of the board, if you divide the board vertically.

RANK: The horizontal lines on a chessboard are called ranks and are referred to as 1st through 8th.

RATED: The United States Chess Federation and FIDE both give ratings to tournament players. Ratings are numbers that go up and down based on whether you win or lose, and against whom.

RELATIVE PIN: A pin where the piece in the middle *could* move legally, but it's not a good idea, because you'll lose what's behind it.

RIVER OF PAWNS: The direction the center pawn chain is facing (king-side or queenside).

SACRIFICE: To give something up to get something better in return.

SCORESHEET: Also called notation paper, this is where you write down all the moves in your game.

SKEWER: A tactic where three pieces are in a row, like a pin, but the more valuable piece is in the middle.

SMOTHERED MATE: A checkmate that happens when a king is trapped by its own pieces and a knight gives the checkmate.

STALEMATE: This is a type of draw. It's very specific: the king is not in check at the moment, but the player has no legal moves. No piece can move but it isn't checkmate.

STRATEGY: Any move or series of moves that helps get your pieces to better squares. Castling is a good strategy, for example.

TACTIC: This is different from a strategy in that it is an immediate way to win material or the game by using a trick, such as a double attack.

TEMPO: "Time" in Latin. If you "gain a tempo" you are doing two things at the same time. For example, if you develop and give check at the same time, you are gaining a tempo.

THREEFOLD REPETITION OF POSITION: If your position has occurred three times, it is a drawn game. In a tournament, you claim the threefold repetition just before you are about to complete the move that makes the position the same for the third time. These positions do *not* need to be in order; they just have to be the same position three times. If even one pawn is in a different spot, then you cannot claim a draw.

TRADE: This is when pieces of equal value are both captured from each side.

UNDERPROMOTION: When a pawn reaches the other side of the board and turns into something other than a queen.

USCF: The United States Chess Federation is an organization where you can become a member, get a monthly magazine, and become eligible to play in any USCF tournament—and you'll get a rating!

WALL: Pawns that are next to each other create a wall. Two pawns next to each other attack four squares in front of them.

WORLD CHAMPION: This person has won the title by winning the World Championship tournament. Will you be the next World Champion?

INDEX

K

Kasparov, Garry, 100
Kings, 7, 30–33
Kingside, 44
Knights, 5, 27–29, 33
Kreiman, Boris, 106–107
Krush, Irina, 80

L

Ladder mate, 41, 54–57, 61
Lapinski, Jerzy, 108–109
Long-range pieces, 19–20

M

Marache, Napoleon, 102
Marco, Georg, 104
Material, 9
MBC (move, block, or
    capture), 39, 47, 73
Menchik, Vera, 97–99
Middle game, 25, 52–53
Miniatures, 108
Mistakes, 104
Morphy, Paul, 53, 102

N

Nakamura, Hikaru, 90–91
Notation, 3, 62–69

O

Openings, 25, 49–51, 87

P

Passed pawns, 16
Patterns, 55–57
Pawns, 4, 13–16, 33
Pins, 20, 76–80, 95

Points, 12

Points, 12
Polgár, Judit, 103
Position, 9–10
Practicing, 115, 118
Promotion, 13, 46–47, 61
Protected pieces, 52
Pushing wood, 113

Q

Queen dance, 58–61
Queens, 6, 23–26, 33
Queenside, 44–45

R

Rainbow opening, 50–51
Ranks, 3
Relative pins, 76–78
Removing the guard, 91–95
Resigning, 103–104
Réti, Richard, 49
River of pawns, 100
Rooks, 5, 17–18, 33

S

Sacrifices, 86, 88–90, 95
Sánchez, Luis Augusto, 93
Scholar's mate, 110–112
Shirov, Alexei, 103, 108–109
Skewers, 20, 81–83, 95
Smothered mate, 29, 89
Stalemate, 46, 58
Stefanova, Antoaneta,
    92–93
Strategies, 71, 96
    castling early, 108–110
    controlling the board,
        97–100, 113
    going for a quick
        checkmate, 110–113
    thinking ahead, 105–107,
        113

using all your pieces,
    101–104, 113
Swallow's tail (checkmate),
    41

T

Tactics, 20, 71, 83–88
    discovered attacks, 20,
        83–88, 95
    forks, 28, 73–76, 95
    pins, 20, 76–80, 95
    removing the guard,
        91–95
    sacrifices, 86, 88–90, 95
    skewers, 20, 81–83, 95
Threefold repetition of
    position, 63
Topalov, Veselin, 101
Tournaments, 116–118
Trading, 9

U

Underpromotion, 46
United States Chess
    Federation (USCF), 116,
    118

W

Walls, 14
Weakest squares, 51
Winning, 8, 12

X

X3D Fritz, 100
X-rays, 81. See also
    Skewers

Y

Yifan, Hou, 92

ABOUT THE AUTHOR

Jessica E. Martin is a chess instructor, author, director, small-business owner, artist, and mother, and she is getting her MFA in poetry at Queens University. She lives in Davidson, North Carolina, and bicycles to chess clubs to teach. She runs local chess tournaments, especially for beginners. She is always interested in learning new things—currently, she's into baking bread, Buddhism, and playing the ukulele. Her main goal is to motivate children to play chess and have fun while building self-confidence. She also works to increase the number of girls, women, and underserved communities competing in chess. Her website is overthechessboard.com.